Contesting Moralities

New Directions in Romani Studies

Editors:
Huub van Baar, Leuven University
Angéla Kóczé, Central European University

Romani Studies has emerged as an interdisciplinary field that offers perspectives derived from the humanities and social sciences in the context of state and transnational institutions. One of the series' aims is to remove the stigma surrounding Roma scholarship, to engage with the controversies regarding Roma identity and, in this way, counter anti-Roma racism. This series publishes innovative, critical, and interdisciplinary scholarship, both in monographs and in edited collections. *New Directions in Romani Studies* includes within its scope migration and border studies, ethnicity studies, anthropology, cultural studies, postcolonial and decolonial studies and gender and queer studies.

Volume 5
CONTESTING MORALITIES: ROMA IDENTITIES, STATE AND KINSHIP
Iliana Sarafian

Volume 4
TEXTURES OF BELONGING: SENSES, OBJECTS AND SPACES OF ROMANIAN ROMA
Andreea Racleş

Volume 3
THE ROMA AND THEIR STRUGGLE FOR IDENTITY IN CONTEMPORARY EUROPE
Edited by Angéla Kóczé and Huub van Baar

Volume 2
INWARD LOOKING: THE IMPACT OF MIGRATION ON ROMANIPE FROM THE ROMANI PERSPECTIVE
Aleksandar G. Marinov

Volume 1
ROMA ACTIVISM: REIMAGINING POWER AND KNOWLEDGE
Edited by Sam Beck and Ana Ivasiuc

CONTESTING MORALITIES
Roma Identities, State and Kinship

Iliana Sarafian

berghahn
NEW YORK · OXFORD
www.berghahnbooks.com

First published in 2023 by
Berghahn Books
www.berghahnbooks.com

© 2023 Iliana Sarafian

Library of Congress Cataloging-in-Publication Data

Names: Sarafian, Iliana, author.
Title: Contesting moralities : Roma identities, state and kinship / Iliana
  Sarafian.
Description: New York : Berghahn Books, 2023. | Series: New directions in Romani
  studies ; volume 5 | Includes bibliographical references and index.
Identifiers: LCCN 2022054582 (print) | LCCN 2022054583 (ebook) | ISBN
  9781800739062 (hardback) | ISBN 9781800739079 (ebook)
Subjects: LCSH: Romanies--Ethnic identity. | Romanies--Cultural
  assimilation. | Romanies--Politics and government.
Classification: LCC DX145 .S23 2023 (print) | LCC DX145 (ebook) | DDC
  305.8914/97--dc23/eng/20230124
LC record available at https://lccn.loc.gov/2022054582
LC ebook record available at https://lccn.loc.gov/2022054583

British Library Cataloguing in Publication Data
A catalogue record for this book is available from the British Library

ISBN 978-1-80073-906-2 hardback
ISBN 978-1-80073-907-9 ebook

https://doi.org/10.3167/9781800739062

To my daughter, with love

The funding for the completion of this book was generously provided by the Centre for Public Authority and International Development at the Firoz Lalji Institute for Africa at the London School of Economics and Political Science (ES/W00786X/1)

Firoz Lalji Institute
for Africa

CONTENTS

Illustrations

❀ ❀ ❀

ACKNOWLEDGEMENTS

This work was possible through the wonderful willingness of the people who kindly shared their stories with me. To them all, I will always be grateful – *Te aven sare bahtale!* I am indebted to Dr Frances Pine, who empowered me with care and advice in the best and worst of times. Dr Paloma Gay y Blasco has been an inspiration, and I am thankful for her timely and invaluable insights. I would not have written this book without the key influence of Professor Judith Okely, who encouraged me to become an anthropologist. I am grateful to The Centre for Public Authority and International Development at the Firoz Lalji Institute for Africa at the London School of Economics and Political Science for generously providing me with the resources and the time to complete this book.

I owe much to my caring parents, sisters, aunts, uncles and friends who gave me all that I needed to be where I am. I lost my grandmother, my uncle and my mother while writing this book and I keep a loving memory of them as the epitome of grace, care and sincerity. I am always grateful to my husband for his unwavering support. This book is dedicated to my daughter in the hope that one day she will explore her diverse ancestry, including her Roma heritage. Last, but not least, I thank God for His provision.

Notes on Terminology and Language

I avoid the term 'Gypsy' throughout the book, and I only use it in the instances of direct quotation or where it is necessary for the discussion. 'Gypsy' (and its translation in Bulgarian as *tsiganin*) is generally considered to be a pejorative exonym within the context of Bulgaria, therefore when I use the word 'Gypsy' I refer to the racialisation process through which a single identity is constructed. However, this work recognises that Roma are a heterogeneous community with linguistic and religious diversity, and there are contexts such as those of the Traveller and Gypsy communities in the United Kingdom in which the use of the term 'Gypsy' is preferable. I acknowledge also that the term 'the Roma', although used as a self-appellation of an ethnocultural subgroup, is used as an 'umbrella' term for Gitanos, Travellers, Romanlar, Kale, Manush and others. Therefore, to avoid grouping, an assumption of a monolithic identity and ascription, I differentiate between 'the Roma' and 'Roma'. I use the latter throughout the book.

Non-English language terms are italicised and translated in the text. Bulgarian, Turkish and Romani words are transliterated in the text also. The words *tsiganin* (for male) and *tsiganka* (for female) are translated as 'Gypsy' in English; however, this does not represent the original pejorative meaning of *tsiganin* and *tsiganka*.

INTRODUCTION
Unexpected Beginnings

Radost

The Roma neighbourhood is located on the outskirts of the town of Radost, close to an industrial sector. The division and separateness from the rest of the neighbourhoods in Radost are seen from the moment I draw close to the Roma quarter. Structurally, the Roma settlement is not autonomous, but there is a clear spatial delineation between the Roma and non-Roma parts of town. It is as if the main town has retreated to its site and the Roma have created their own site. While there are a few Roma living outside the Roma neighbourhood – mainly in the apartment blocks near the neighbourhood – the majority of Roma live here. There are approximately 1,300 people in the quarter. Doctors and nurses visit rarely, if at all. Teachers visit before enrolment time at the beginning of the school year to make sure they have the required quota of pupils. When social workers visit the neighbourhood, inhabitants are worried about their children being taken away into care. Police navigate only the main road, since going further into the neighbourhood is perceived as dangerous. The rubbish trucks come once a month and when prompted by a concerned Roma citizen. Ironically, all the rubbish bin collectors and the cleaners in Radost are Roma.

In the 1950s, there were only a handful of Roma families in the old Roma settlement of Radost. This is when the local administration decided to move them to a new area, close to the industrial part of town. The old Roma neighbourhood was next to the site on which a health facility was going to be built. First, it was called 'Newcomers', then 'New Road', and later it was renamed again after a local wood factory merged with the Roma neighbourhood. Everyone in Radost, including the inhabitants of the neighbourhood, refer to it as the *mahala*. In official documents, however, the name of the neighbourhood is presented as either *tsiganski* (Gypsy), *romski* or 'New Road' neighbourhood.

Since the fall of communism in 1989, there has been little investment in the area, with poor infrastructure, no pavements and no streetlights. Apparently, the roads have names, but there are no street signs or labels; an outsider would not likely be able to reach their destination without asking the locals. It is no surprise that the roads are not signposted, as the neighbourhood's name, 'New Road', gives a clue – there is a perpetual newness to this Roma quarter and its 'newcomer' citizens, although the site has existed for over seventy years.

As I walk into the neighbourhood, I notice that the streets gradually become narrower. The rubbish tanks at the beginning of the neighbourhood are overflowing, and I wonder when the last collection took place. The effect is not only visual; I can smell it in the air along with burned wood and animal waste as I walk along the main street. I see houses, most of them unfinished but painted with bright colours. Here and there, I see trees, a reminder of better days gone by. There are no trees further down into the neighbourhood. Some of the houses have broken or missing windows covered with carpet or blankets; the gates are broken, and the roofs have holes in the metal or broken tiles. My eye catches a white building with a well-maintained façade, a painted fence and a cross on its roof. The Roma evangelical church is standing in contrast with the rest of the grey and unkempt buildings.

Further towards the central part of the neighbourhood, I see a space burgeoning with children and resembling a children's playground. This playground is next to one of the busiest roads in town, leading to the industrial site. Most children are here without their parents' permission because the playground is without a fence and has open access to the busy main road. Cars, lorries, horse carts and people pass by constantly. The children fight with each other over the one broken swing left and a metal piece resembling a spaceship. On both sides of the busy road, I see men waiting in the hope of being picked up by local businessmen for temporary daily work.

A short street takes me to the central part of the neighbourhood – a square space with a stone floor covered with cigarette butts and empty waffle and sweet packages. It is a space filled with adults and children – a beehive in this afternoon hour. I see a two-story building, in front of which is a café. The first floor is used as a *chitalishte* (a house of culture). This building was erected by Roma volunteers during communist times. There are many makeshift market stalls with second-hand clothes, fruit and vegetables. I hear negotiations between customers and traders. In the summer evenings, the square is filled with people who sit on the warm stones, drinking beer and eating sunflower seeds. Children chase around late into the night.

Beyond the central part of the neighbourhood, I see a labyrinth of narrow unpaved roads. Two small cars cannot pass by each other. These muddy roads are there to teach me that next time I will need better shoes. I can see why children have given up on wearing shoes; walking shoeless in the mud may be easier. I feel for the children who arrive at school covered in mud every morning. As I progress ahead on a narrow road, I go through different smells. Someone is cooking, and they are calling their children to come and eat. I hear all kinds of sounds – mostly the latest hit music. This neighbourhood is anything but silent. People are watching me. I am foreign here. I ask a stranger where Neli, the teacher, lives, and they show me. I stop in front of the house I was looking for, and Neli meets me. This place will be home for the next few months.

The introduction to the locals in Radost was important. My parents insisted on accompanying me on my first visit to Radost. I did not see their safety concerns as relevant, since I had just come back home from living on my own in London – surely, I was going to manage. However, I failed to remember that for an unmarried thirty-year-old Roma woman to live with a family that is not her kin was highly unusual. My parents knew this detail, and their presence in Radost had a purpose; they were there to protect their daughter's respectability. My parents were identified as Roma, and this gave me a good start. However, being identified as Roma was insufficient. I had to be presented as a respectable daughter. So, Neli's father and mother took on the responsibility of looking after me. By living with them, I was automatically recognised as a member of their family. In fact, I was later introduced as a distant relative.

I got to know Neli through my connection with a nongovernmental organisation based in another larger Roma neighbourhood in Bulgaria. Neli was employed as a teacher by the NGO that provided education support for Roma children in the region. Like me, Neli was in her thirties, unmarried and educated. Neli's family kindly offered me the role of a daughter, and this meant that I took part in almost every aspect of family life. I lived in a household of ten – Neli's parents, their two sons, two daughters-in-law, three grandchildren, Neli and myself. Neli's mother looked after the grandchildren, the men sold clothes in the local flea market, and the daughters-in-law went to work in the local sewing factory. I alternated between helping Neli with her education projects, childcare and doing chores in the house. The cooking, the cleaning, the childcare and the shopping were entirely women's domains. The men, on the other hand, went out to the market early in the morning and came back home at dusk. Neli's sisters-in-law competed with each other as to who would make the tastiest food dishes, mainly pastries and cakes, and Neli's mother would comment on their skills. Gradually, my cooking skills had to be tested as well. 'Iliana, you must learn to be a good homemaker. People look for hard-working daughters-in-law.' So, I made *banitsa*, baklava, beans and potato soup, fruit compote and cooked with anything that the garden produced.

Being unmarried gave me the immediate position of a daughter, but since I was significantly older than the unmarried Roma girls in the neighbourhood, I had a somewhat ambiguous position within the community. I mostly associated with the women in the family, and I had to abide by the established gender rules; however, as an unmarried woman everyone, both men and women, saw me as not mature enough, hence not entirely belonging to the gender categories established in the household and the community. I did not have children, who defined the most important role of a woman, and hence I was not entirely viewed as an accomplished person. My position was somewhere between a girl-child and a woman. Of course, this status had its advantages and disadvantages. Themes such as childcare, the family economy, education, health and discrimination were openly discussed with me by all. However, I was cut off from the area of sexuality, marriage and intimate relationships. For instance, one of the topics of the women's meetings in the local church concerned intimacy, the prevention of violence and HIV/AIDS. A colleague of Neli's working on this topic in the NGO was invited to give a talk to the women in the community. Neli gently warned me that this topic may not be so relevant for me and swiftly left the meeting. I, on the other hand, thought that my presence would not be noticed. In a few minutes, the pastor's wife whispered in my ear 'Iliana, it may be better if you are not part of this session. I am sure one day you will be able to participate.' My innocence and expected ignorance on the subject had to be protected along with my reputation.

People often wondered why I was in the neighbourhood. My Roma origin and past became the subject of many discussions. Whose daughter was I? Where did I come from? Why was I not married? Although in time both the researcher and my Roma-ness gained me entry into the corridors of state institutions and the homes of the Roma neighbourhood, being a Roma insider meant that my reputation was of utmost importance to deal with first. My childhood was spent in a Roma neighbourhood, leaving me intimately aware of the locals' worldview and social norms, and I was credulously certain that this experience would give me quick and unproblematic access. Precisely because of this intimate involvement over a substantial portion of my life, I believed that there was an underlying shared experience that enabled me to appreciate the local contexts over and above mere understanding (Okely and Callaway 1992). Ultimately, I was an insider, but soon I realised how naive my belief was. Living in Radost challenged my perceptions and expectations because being accepted by the local community was more complex than I had imagined.

Writing a book was not a sufficient reason for a single Roma woman to leave her parents behind, so most people in the neighbourhood assumed that I was in Radost to help Neli with her education projects. Initially, Neli's family thought that I was running away from home because of something else, other than just writing a book. Neli's mother asked me quietly one day, 'Did you have something bad happen to you? My Neli went out with a Bulgarian boy and then they separated, and look at her now struggling to find a good man.' Neli's mother undertook the role of making sure that all her neighbours and hence the neighbourhood knew that I was a respectable girl by teaching me how to cook and look after the household, in addition to telling people that I would write a book and help with Neli's work.

Sastipe

Eight months into my life in Radost, I had to interrupt my research as both of my parents were going through major illnesses and needed care. I needed a longer period of study interruption, which meant that I lost my studentship bursary and needed to fund my research on my own. No matter how precise and 'scientific' my research plan was, its implementation was dependent on innumerable and unexpected contingencies. On my return, Neli had married, and she was living in another, larger city in Bulgaria. Neli's brothers and their wives had immigrated to the UK, and Neli's parents were preparing to join them to help with childcare. In fact, a large number of Roma in Radost had moved abroad, mainly to Italy, Germany and the UK. By this time, I was also married and had a baby. Without Neli's family, my return to Radost was impossible logistically. I needed different accommodation and childcare. However, what seemed impossible to me at the time was not impossible for Neli, who invited me to visit her in the city of Sastipe.

Sastipe is a large city in Bulgaria with a Roma population of approximately 3,000 people. The Roma neighbourhood is unofficially structured into different quarters or *mahalas*, as the locals call them – the Lower and the Upper sites. The inhabitants of the Lower mahala are both Roma and non-Roma, and the buildings there are tall and separated into family units. Most of the streets are paved and clean. Many of the Roma inhabitants of the Lower mahala refer to themselves as Turks and speak Turkish. The spatial separation of the two parts of the Sastipe Roma neighbourhood can be traced back to the formation of the first Roma neighbourhoods in Bulgaria during the Ottoman rule and is based on the differentiation of ethnic but mostly religiously homogeneous neighbourhoods (Asenov 2018: 89). Today the separation between Sastipe's Lower and Upper Roma neighbourhood is largely due to differences in economic access. Most of the residents of the

Upper mahala have Bulgarian names and moved to Sastipe from other parts of the country as opposed to the more established long-term residents of the Lower mahala, who refer to each other with Turkish names and are believed to have come to the neighbourhood with the Ottomans hundreds of years ago.

The physical difference between the two sides is visible. A significant share of the inhabitants of the Lower mahala work in Germany and the Netherlands, where they have established connections with Turkish communities as they can speak the Turkish language. Working abroad guarantees them a stable and higher income. The Lower mahala is well connected to the rest of the city, with closer access to schools, shops and amenities, as opposed to the Upper mahala, which is smaller in size and is located in the so-called 'unregulated part' of the city. This means that the buildings do not exist in the municipality register, hence electricity and water are not provided, and wherever there are amenities they are seen as part of temporary dwellings by the local authorities. The area and its people are associated with danger, dirt, violence and immorality. The Upper and the Lower sites intermix rarely in everyday life; however, marriages between the inhabitants of the two sites happen, and local churches consist of inhabitants from both sites.

I had relatives in Sastipe with whom I could stay and who could help me look after my baby, and this is how I embarked on the next phase of my research. Having become a mother when I continued my research in Sastipe gave me greater entry into the women's world. The presence of my baby daughter also generated much interest amongst my interlocutors, and it shaped the research process and its findings. Writing a book was not sufficient for Sastipe's Roma, and for them I had to be what anthropology calls 'an engaged anthropologist', whereby one conducts engaged research involving collaboration, advocacy and activism (Marcus 2012; Ortner 2019). When I joined Neli in Sastipe, she had established a mother's initiative that was part of the local evangelical church and consisted of attendants from both mahalas. They were mostly young mothers, who were my first informants in Sastipe. Gradually, I was invited to their homes and took part in everyday household tasks as well as in events such as weddings, funerals, child dedications and church services.

Structure of the Book

Influenced by a situational approach, the written materials presented here range from personal accounts to descriptions of locations and reproduced stories. Thus, I opened this book with an introduction to the locations of my research. Radost and Sastipe are different in size, composition and economic access, although there are natural 'partial connections' (Strathern 2004) and remarkable similarities in narratives and identity signifiers.[1] So, in the chapters of this book I have attempted to capture life experiences, the meaning, the geo-symbolism and the place-making within these landscapes and beyond them. By introducing the two Roma neighbourhoods, I would like to recognise the role of space in the lifeworlds of my informants and to introduce the reader to marginal urban geographies, where the work, control and withdrawal of the state can be best captured (Fassin 2015).

The relationships between identification and my research sites interrelate in important ways. The themes are directly influenced by where my informants live, including the question of by whom are Roma histories controlled; how children are brought up and who influences their education; how economic and social transformation takes place; who becomes 'the Roma elite'; who looks after Roma children in state institutions; and how womanhood and adulthood begin and are negotiated. Distance, location and topography relate to all themes discussed in this book and just like the Roma neighbourhoods are always perceived as incomplete or in a perpetual state of newness, removal and reconstruction; the stories I present are also unfinished. On purpose, each chapter provides only an entrance into multiple worlds, hoping to direct attention to the story of the people concerned as individuals with agency, as humans, which is what the very word 'Roma' means – to be a person and a human. By presenting a singularity of individual trajectories, situatedness, voices and their specific circumstance, I explore Roma lives from unexpected standpoints. This unexpected and contradictory nature of the minutiae of everyday lives manifests across different arenas: from history and kinship to childhood and gender relationships.

Each chapter brings forward different spaces, stories, domains and contradictions in order to explore the processes through which they are made possible. Ultimately, identity politics arises as a result of representation in space, history and culture; therefore, it is not so much about 'who we are' or 'where we came from' as it is about 'who we might become' (Hall 1996a; 1996b). This latter aspect is considered in the stories that make up this work. Importantly, I aim at narrowing the gaze at a selection of undercurrent themes resonating in contemporary Romani studies but which I felt needed to be explored further.

The complex undercurrent theme that glues everything together and that runs throughout the book is identification and how it is impinged on by the role of the state and its various degrees of interaction with kinship. The presence of the state ranges from implementing explicit interventionist policies and prosaic micro control to what seems to be a withdrawal and retreat. In the first chapters of the book, the state features as the main player in decision-making, in historicising, educating and taking care of Roma children, and in the later chapters the state's presence in communal kinship and gender is somewhat sporadic and withdrawn yet still there in the background through the norms it promotes. Each chapter provides examples of how kinship opposes the state to create alternative narratives and forms of morality, history, identity and belonging. The two of course are interconnected. Kinship and state politics go hand in hand (Thelen and Alber 2018). These spaces of state presence or absence, relationships inside and outside the community and the state, and ways and choices of identification, can present opportunities to learn. Herein lies the broader contribution of this book, namely its invitation to the reader to consider the unpredictability, the 'world of multiple orderings of reality' (Tambiah 1990: 84), the incommensurability and unexpectedness of the everyday that animates human lives by following Roma individual trajectories and their interconnectedness with a partial, non-unitary and embodied state, the one administered by teachers, social workers, activists, medical workers and others.

The book is structured in a way that follows the intensity of regimes of power, or as I call them 'moralities', in emic terms, and which I distinguish between in accordance with their corresponding domains and how they play out in individual lives. This work is not only about the 'inside' Roma world but also about the values, the affects, the persons, the contradictions and moral subjectivities of the state. I set the scene by introducing the history of my interlocutors and by exploring what being Roma may imply for children and adults who grew up on the edges of the community, or outside, specifically in care, and of Roma whose lives may be seen to contradict or challenge expectations of both Roma and non-Roma. These accounts present individuals and collective actors in interaction in everyday life, in the neighbourhood and in institutional and state settings, including educational settings, away from the Roma neighbourhood and under the influence of macro and micro politics of the state. I gradually build up the theme of kinship in each chapter to show its practicality and interrelationship with the work of the state. Towards the end of the book, I reflect on what are seen as the 'typical' internal markers of identification such as marriage, weddings and gender positionality and the enormous importance they carry as well as the challenges they pose inside and outside the communities of my research. These are classical themes in Romani ethnographies, but I have aimed to present them with a twist whereby they are no longer a window into the world of rules and tradition but into the possibilities and impossibilities of planning a future, creating or unmaking a community, of strategic kinship, individuality, agency, socioeconomic survival and striving to be.

Note

1. Radost and Sastipe are pseudonyms and throughout this work, for reasons of confidentiality, I utilise geospatial obfuscation or combine stories from both locations. I also refer to all inhabitants by names different from their own.

CHAPTER 1

ANALYTICAL APPROACH
Identity, State and Kinship

One childhood memory springs to mind as I reflect on my impetus to question identification. It was a hot day in August during the school holidays. Everyone in my Bulgarian Roma neighbourhood was inside their homes, having an afternoon nap or watching Latin American telenovelas. Now and then, one would hear the laughter of children sprinkling each other with cold water in the scorching sun. I was at home with my two sisters, watching a Bollywood movie, when suddenly we heard our neighbour shouting for help. Tanko was in distress because his pregnant wife Milena was not well. Milena was my friend, and we went to school together; she was also my neighbour, and we grew up almost inseparably. Aged sixteen, Milena left school to marry Tanko. That afternoon, Tanko knocked on our window and asked whether he could use my parents' phone to call an ambulance. At the time, my parents' house was one of only a handful of houses in the neighbourhood with a stationary telephone line. I opened the door and Tanko rushed past me to pick up the phone. He uttered his address, and I could hear the frustration in his voice growing until he was screaming at the people on the other end of the line. 'I need an ambulance! She cannot breathe. I don't have a car! I can't bring her to you.' The ambulance never arrived, and Milena was taken to hospital in the car of another neighbour. She gave birth to a baby girl, and later she passed away.

Identity

Milena's story has remained firmly anchored in my memory, and it has prompted me to ask questions about the division between 'them' and 'us'. This identity typification, as in Milena's case, where Roma women are seen as perpetually pregnant and giving birth to multitudes of children at a young age (I come back to this in Chapter 6), or what was supposed to be Roma and non-Roma, influenced people's daily lives and their deservingness of support – be it medical or otherwise. I was disappointed and perplexed. Growing up, I was painfully aware of the daily struggles of my community, and this led me to a preoccupation with issues of identity and morality. My own sense of identity was entrenched in the experience of discrimination and the fight against it.

Many times the culture with which I thought I was familiar presented some puzzles and unknowns. As I went through various stages of activism, and in the course of my research, I found spaces, stories and examples of the everyday that challenged my preconceptions about Roma identification. It is apparent in the narratives presented here that there is an enduring appeal of dichotomies between Roma and non-Roma, state and nonstate, public and private, and I engage with these categories, hierarchies and inequalities by giving examples of how they are entangled and connected and complement each other. I also pay attention to unexpected issues, including the challenges of my 'insider' identification, which presented me with opportunities to observe and learn. I provide glimpses of the unexpected and positions of liminality, 'neither here, nor there' and of 'betwixt and between' (Turner 1967). This 'in-betweenness' (Basu 2017) opposes methodological essentialism, the singular, the certain and fixed classifications of Roma identification, which I thought I knew so intimately. I found Edward Said's writings on how imperialism has impacted identities helpful: 'no one today is purely one thing. Labels like Indian, or woman, or Muslim, or American are not more than starting-points' (Said 1993: 336). The people of my research dealt with principles and behaviours that contradict what is widely perceived to be 'typical' of Roma and community belonging. Following this logic, I found myself asking questions about the exceptions of the 'expected' and how these are navigated inside Roma communities and externally.

I must note that it is not my intention to present a coherent and conclusive response to the questions I ask. Indeed, this is not an account of what constitutes Roma identities, nor do I set out to explore what is unique for the communities of my research. There are numerous studies that have focused on elaborating Roma identification, and I capitalise on this work in order to position my work and its contribution. My intent is to present situations of permanent 'unfinishedness' (Biehl and Locke 2017), to create episodes that do not necessarily make 'one whole' of a linear account that paints one picture; rather I attempt to bring together a collage of experiences and stories with which I hope to challenge 'the expected' and the categorical in order to stimulate further discussions. In this pursuit, I found that the 'anthropology of becoming' (Biehl and Locke 2010; Deleuze 1995) is particularly relevant.

An 'anthropology of becoming' stipulates the illumination of the everyday through the singularity of human experience, 'experience in the making', through ethnography that does not assume universality in theory, writing that does not reduce but hopes to convey the 'messiness of the social world and the real struggles in which our informants and their kin are involved' (Biehl and Locke 2010: 321). Such writing contends that despite the importance of theories for understanding human experience they have limits and can only attempt to interpret the messiness of life partially (Jackson 2013).

Thus, the core analytical idea of this work is that Roma identification can be intricate and at times problematic alongside, through, and despite the constraining circumstantial external and internal communal forces. I follow the plot of individuals to identify the many juxtaposed contexts through which identification in social life is empirically negotiated. My aim is to paint the complex, uneven nature of inequality and identification, which here I mostly refer to as identity, and of the ways, individuals confront, negotiate and reproduce understandings and demands that are often conflicting, ambiguous and contradictory. Speaking of identity here, I do not reject Hall's (1996b: 2) suggestion that the term identification must be preferable to identity itself; on the contrary, I agree that the term identification allows for a better understanding of the process in which people come to identify themselves and that identification 'happens over time that is never absolutely stable' (Hall 1996b). Here I am transgressing and using identification and identity interchangeably whereby identity is both situational as located in the social context, a question of blood and inherited traits from generation to generation, as well as a constantly evolving unstable and fluid notion.

The social science literature on Roma has tended to present identity as monolithic and given, as opposed to being fragmented and ambiguous. Well-known anthropological studies that I draw upon in this work have engaged in elaborating a shared group identity whereby the individual is seen primarily as part of the collective and communal whole (Engebrigtsen 2007; Gay y Blasco 1999, 2008; Gheorghe 1997; Lemon 2000; Okely 1983, 1994; Silverman 1988). These important accounts have laid the foundation of Romani studies today and focus largely on what may be expected of Roma, in order to make sense of group belonging. Nevertheless, authors have also pointed to the contradictory nature of categorisation and that in practice its application is constantly contested (Gay y Blasco 2011; Gay y Blasco and Hernández 2020; Stewart 2013; Theodosiou 2008; Williams 2003): 'in treating individuals primarily as exemplars ... the ethnographic literature consistently describes them [Roma] as amorphous aggregates of archetypes, groups of moral beings equally positioned vis-à-vis the world' (Gay y Blasco 2011: 445).

As it happened, in the process of writing this book, I questioned my focus on Roma identification. Despite my (at times obsessive) interest in the subject, I found the topic to be too complex, highly contested and politicised. Roma identification is complex because of the heterogeneity and difference in subgroup identity. There is a variety of religious, geographical and other differences and affiliations that divide Roma groups in Europe. Acton and Klimova (2001) record that Roma are often seen as a 'nation without a state'. It is challenging to talk about Roma *per se* because the term encompasses a wide variety of subgroups. Roma cannot be seen as a homogenous community but rather as 'communities of shared social practices' (Guy 2001), and although there are similarities in speaking the Romani language (Matras 2013), in cultural practices, rituals and belief systems (Fosztó 2006; Gay y Blasco 2001; Ries 2011; Roman 2015), there is a multitude of differences such as geographical location, languages and preference for self-identification (Fremlova 2022; McGarry 2010). In Bulgaria also, as in much of Europe, Roma are generally seen as a single and homogeneous community in the public discourse (Tomova 2008).

Numerous studies have been engaged in explaining who 'the Roma' are. Linguists, for example, have based their scholarship on the link between the Romani language and the Indo-Aryan languages of India (Matras 2002). Historically, Roma have been seen as nomadic tribes who migrate from place to place because of their 'itinerant handicrafts' (Bancroft 2001). After frictions and mutual intolerance between 'settled and unsettled', the so called 'nomads' must escape to another location in order to survive. In time as well as in space this 'unsettled' lifestyle' had to 'move on' (Kenrick and Clark 1999). Roma, Gypsies and Travellers had to adapt to the 'Gadge/gorgio'[1] world constantly, to negotiate and adapt to the dominant economic patterns and 'know the enemy' and interpret this knowledge in order to be self-sufficient (Okely 2011: 42). According to Eriksen (2002: 74), Roma are 'a cultural and symbolic phenomenon' viewed through the prism of difference. As Barany et al. (2002: 14) put it, 'the most important factor of Gypsiness is the division of the world into *Roma* and *gadje*, a division that has contributed to the absence of a large-scale integration of Roma into mainstream societies'. This significant factor for negotiating Roma-ness is the re-creation of Roma culture vis-à-vis other cultures, or the emphasis of particular choices Roma make in positioning themselves versus the dominant population.

There is a consensus amongst anthropologists that Roma identity is created as a result of and in opposition to the macro-community (Gay y Blasco 1999; Marushiakova and Popov 2005; Okely 1994; Stewart 1997). In other words, identification (or Roma-ness, Romanipe, Gypsiness, Gitaneidad, etc.) is grounded in the difference between Roma and non-Roma as well as between Roma subgroups. For example, Silverman (1988) presents the case of 'Gypsiness' with the example of Roma in North America, who succeeded in preserving distinct cultural attributes by maintaining boundaries between Roma and non-Roma through mobility, employment and abiding by strict taboo systems. Later, Silverman (2012: 53) also argued that Roma identity 'has always been construed in relation to hegemonic powers such as patrons of the arts, socialist ideologies, European Union officials, and NGO funders'. Gay y Blasco's work on Gitanos in Spain shows that Roma differentiate themselves from *Payos* (non-Roma) by referring to women's decency and chastity. It would be a failure if a woman does not adhere to the established rules of morality (1999: 63).

Durst (2011) in 'What Makes Us Gypsies, Who Knows ... ?!' contends that the category of Roma/Gypsy is one that acquires its meaning through the relationship with non-Roma, confirming earlier writings. Surdu (2014: 33), a Roma scholar, goes on to say that 'the Roma population is a negative and oppositional construction made by dominant groups and self-internalised by many of those labelled as Roma'. Mirga (2018), himself also Roma, confronts Surdu's approach by advocating for a more active engagement with research on how Roma shape their own ethnogenesis and by considering the views of the emerging Roma scholars on the subject of identification. Perhaps Stewart and Rovid (2011: 426) give an answer to this tension of essentialism versus social constructionism in stating that 'our notions of culture, of an ethnic group or people are so utterly rooted in the schemas derived from practices of nation-states (which are or at least strive to be, homogenous, neatly bounded entities) that Romany communities appear as an anomaly' (ibid.: 2).

Other authors have employed a socio-historical approach to investigate Roma identities through the lens of poverty, precariousness and the concept of 'underclass' (Ladányi and Szelényi 2003). Studies have accounted for the effects of communism on Roma in Eastern Europe (Gheorghe 1997; Guy 2001; Mirga and Gheorghe 1997; Sigona and Trehan 2009) and contended that communist approaches to Roma assimilation produced ethnicising and politicisation of the respective Roma communities and that this dictated how they identify today. Authors have also focused on Roma political representation (Surdu and Kovats 2015; Van Baar 2011), including the aspect of transnationality, representation in Europe, policy and identity (Vermeersch 2001). Concepts such as 'Roma integration' and 'social inclusion' in the political arena have become the vocabulary of large international nongovernment and government organisations whereby Roma identity is conceptualised as 'ethnoclass' and focuses on the alleviation of poverty and improvement of their socioeconomic situation through education, housing and employment (Vermeersch 2006).

More recent studies have suggested 'super-diversity' (after Vertovec 2007) and echo Okely's earlier suggestion for the cautious use of hybridity[2] as a relevant framework to explain the heterogeneity of Roma communities and discuss identification as less determined – beyond complexity and essentialism (Okely 1994: 62; Tremlett 2014). Kóczé et al. (2018) warn of the provenance of 'super-diversity', hybridity and the 'risk of losing sight of ethnicity' (ibid.: 63). Instead, the authors reaffirm what earlier feminist studies have conceptualised as intersectionality (Collins 2015; Crenshaw 1991; Yuval-Davis 2011) and suggest it as a framework to use when considering Roma identification and its negotiations. Yildiz and DeGenova (2018) challenge the 'status quo' within Romani studies, which has presented a dual approach to theorising 'the Roma' identity. The authors contend that there is an opposition between the essentialisation of Roma identity, 'culture' and 'ethnicity' and denial of the relevance of ethnicity. Along the lines of this thinking, in this work I push beyond these boundaries by providing examples of remarkable similarities – common and shared identification markers, as well as spaces and circumstances – that individuals may identify as Roma or decide not to in choosing to identify differently. For this purpose, I provide context, building on both earlier and more recent research in Romani studies, whilst insisting on the value of the micro, the singular, 'unfinished', 'the non-important' and unexpected identification, whilst disentangling categorisations, aggregates and topology.

State

There is one particular agent, an ingredient, actor as well as spectator present to varying degrees within each chapter and this is the state. So how do I conceptualise 'the state' and its interventions within domains of education, social relations and constructed boundaries such as family, civil society and religion? Abrams (2008) argued that scholars should cease thinking, talking and writing about the state as if it existed as a unified, autonomous moral entity or agent. The institutions of the 'state system' are at the core of studying the state – or in other words, of working out how the state comes to assume its status and authority over all forms of social relations (Ferguson and Gupta 2002). History-making, education, child protection and safeguarding, civil society and religion provide clues to understanding the micropolitics of the work of the state, how state authorities and governments operate in people's daily lives, and how the state comes to be imagined, encountered and reimagined by its subjects. Analytically, arguing against the assumption that 'the state' is an empirical object, Abrams proposed that it is not 'reality which stands behind the mask of political practice' (Abrams 2008: 87).

The state could be reproduced through different practices – that is, bureaucratic practices through which the state's primacy and superiority over other social institutions are reproduced, and social inequalities are maintained (Fassin 2015; Sharma and Gupta 2006). But what is it that the state reproduces? Practically, the state reproduces moralities and affects, both believed and performed, and throughout the book I show that the state's values may not always be shared by its subjects, including its representatives. As opposed to seeing the state as unemotional and monolithic in structure, the examples I give show a series of gaps where the state's presence can become extremely brutal or is in fact absent. For example, in practice, it seems that once a Roma family or a child comes to the attention of social services, there is a high chance that the child may be taken to an institution. The school administration can make decisions regarding a child's education performance while sharing prejudices against Roma parents whose children they educate. The state is seen as the provider of 'better education', 'better nourishment' and 'better upbringing and culture', although usually states are seen as being devoid of culture and are primarily conceptualised in institutional terms (Stoler 2004). Theories of nationalism are often implicit in theories of the state; similarly, theories of nationalism assume that nationalism is a state prerogative (Anderson [1983] 2006). These narratives of nationalism march alongside the concerns for better education and 'enculturation' while the numbers of Roma children labelled as coming from 'inadequate families' continue to rise (Gay y Blasco 2016; Toma 2012).

I must acknowledge that it is easier not to distinguish between the state and the politico-historical regimes (e.g. socialism and postsocialism). I am aware that I need to analyse the state at work and not only as an external and political entity. There is a false dichotomisation of the state and the community/the kin, the grand versus the small, and the external versus the local (Pine 2018; Thelen and Alber 2018). We are warned of the danger of reifying the state as an autonomous entity that regulates the communities we study (Taussig 1997). The many levels, agendas, faces, positions and organisations that constitute the state 'can be both arbitrary and contingent' (Harvey 2005: 139) and need to be conceptualised not only through the lens of the state but also through community frameworks (Fassin 2015; Navaro-Yashin 2002).

Bearing in mind these considerations, I engage with the state in a nuanced manner (I do not imply a monolithic state), reifying its motives while still presenting its major role in Roma identification. I shall show how the state regulates its subjects through mechanisms such as historical accounts, education, care, birth and marriage and how individuals and communities resist, shape and perpetuate culture and identities. In order to achieve this, I consider the challenges and impediments, as well as the coping mechanisms, inside kinship relationships. I argue that gender, childhood, adulthood and parenthood can be understood within a framework of kinship relatedness (Carsten 2000), and I provide examples of how kinship opposes the state in order to create alternative narratives and forms of history, identity and belonging.

I write of the state within the realms of socialism and postsocialism. The collapse of the Soviet Union, its various effects on Central and Eastern European states and the transition towards a free-market economy are important aspects of analysis, and I bring this to the attention of the reader in each chapter. I look at the heralded change in the role of the state and its relationship to kinship and gender roles and how these are inscribed in different institutional settings and practices in Bulgaria. The attempts of the 'transition states' to establish liberal democracies have included some populations and excluded others, and these complexities have shaped people's lives since the fall of communism (Hann 2002; Kaneff 2019; Pine 2018; Verdery 2003).

Kinship

I am concerned with the ways that social and domestic categories, relationships, moralities, authorities and identities intersect with categories created by the state (Carsten 2000; Thelen and Alber 2018). These interactions are observed in the school system, in the neighbourhood, in NGO activism, in marriage strategies and in religious affiliation. Kinship in the book intersects with the choices my informants make to speak about or intentionally forget the past and its effects on family and individuals. Kinship responds to state assimilation, omission of mother tongues, alternative communal histories and persecution. Kinship here is also about the provision of a home, resources and education at the expense of severing relationships. Kinship influences gendered and age strategies, socioeconomic survival, and mutual support between relatives, those connected by blood and those connected because of various life circumstances, beyond the functioning of close family members.

I trace state ideologies that undervalue or even suppress the role of the domestic domain in favour of a particular public one, where Roma families or communities are perceived as antisocial, and where the state is seen as the only provider of social value and authority (Pine 2007, 2018). Similarly, I also write of kinship that has authority to choose – kinship with agency. The narratives presented here point to kinship strategies opposing external, most often state, impositions to create their own spaces of survival and lifeworlds. Kinship in the book starts with the work of the state and its kinning strategies, be it through the work of the education system, the childcare institutions, or through the interactions with NGO activists. The analysis of kinship continues also to incorporate the domestic sphere, the intimate realms of the home, the family, the community and the individual. When investigated, all these aspects introduce different perspectives, ultimately presenting a complex yet understandable story of humans striving to be related and live life to become.

Method and Analysis

The methodology utilised in this work is led by the circumstances of my research. Although I did not plan to conduct a multisited ethnography, the changes in my personal situation and that of my host family resulted in the unintentional multisitedness of my research. Since its beginnings, multisited ethnography has gained traction in anthropology because of its adaptability (Marcus 1995). Multisited ethnography challenges the 'Malinowskian complex' of a single-site ethnography and proposes a methodological shift in ethnographic practice under the influence of the 'writing culture' critique in a postmodern world affected by globalisation (Clifford and Marcus 1986). Multisitedness proposes freedom from conceptual boundaries of the delimited site and allows one to follow movements of people, ideas and objects to trace and map complex networks. I was aware that multisited research has its limitations and arbitrariness (Candea 2007: 168); however, the inevitability of my circumstance pointed me in a direction where the research sites chose me. By following my main contact Neli in the first research location and by tapping into my previous knowledge, language skills and 'epistemological insiderness' (Brubaker 2017) or simply by being an anthropologist 'at home', I forged long-lasting relationships in the field. I had to be open and adapt to the developments occurring, as I realised that the methodological plan I had prepared in my pre-fieldwork year would not enable me to achieve the kind of embodiment, participation and knowledge acquisition I had envisaged. Building on relationships of trust and respectability was more important than the methods I had devised. There is a permanent tension between empirical realities and theories, and I find 'theory to be always catching up to reality' (Biehl and Locke 2017: 7).

Participant observation enabled me to live with and be a part of the daily lives of people, and I questioned my fundamental assumptions in accordance with learned theories or previous experiences. As I created relationships, I chose life histories as narratives to be able to capture experiences. Narratives, stories and songs brought meaning to personal and collective encounters, and they were also transmitters of knowledge and perceived moralities. Through the collection of life histories, I hoped to bring out my informants' understandings of their lived experiences and the ideals, morals and practices attached to them. Nevertheless, life histories or narratives are also constructed; meanings are created from the researcher's experience.

This is in opposition to the positivist theories, which emphasise neutrality and 'detachment' from the object of research. In line with this methodology, I set out to produce reflexive knowledge, a narrative inquiry as a collaborative construction that contains the researcher's perspective. Methodology, theoretical considerations and positionality converge, and I find that in the text ahead I come back to examine the concept of self constantly. Crucially and openly, I ground my methodological approach in an exploration of my own position in the field as a Roma woman, which is carried across from chapter to chapter. Ultimately, it is my hope that the text of this book will convey, if only in part, the voices that I attempted to capture in order to present an ethnographic sensorium of life as lived by the ones that matter the most – those people who shared their stories with me.

Notes

1. The terms 'Gadje', 'Gorgio' (England) or 'Payo' (Spain), 'Country people' (Ireland) and 'Flatties' (Scotland) are used by Roma/Gypsy/Traveller communities to refer to non-Roma. The terms are seen as pejorative.
2. Okely suggests the concept, but she also acknowledges that she hesitates to use it lest it create incongruity.

CHAPTER 2

NARRATING BEGINNINGS
AND MEMORIES

My family rarely talked about where they came from. My own interest in the subject began, admittedly, after I learned about the family history of a friend, who diligently produced an elaborated ancestral family tree going back centuries. My grandmother's memories about where her ancestors came from and what they did were limited, but she nevertheless recalled narratives, some firsthand and others passed down by previous generations, that unveiled details previously not known to me. Some of my ancestors were war soldiers; others fled persecution; some were servants and dreamed of owning land to be able to settle. As in most family histories, there were stories of marriage, separation, single motherhood, death, shame, joy and secrets, many secrets.

I wanted to find out more about my own beginnings, and so I visited my hometown's library, the regional history museums and the national archives. I found the earliest evidence of my family's existence in an archive that recorded persons employed in the 'Labour-Cooperative Farm' (*trudo-vo-kooperativno zemedelsko stopanstvo—*TKZS)[1] in 1945, after the end of the Second World War. There I traced my great grandfather, whose previous profession was recorded as '*tsiganin*' (Gypsy). I was saddened to come across a state mechanism that placed Roma outside the boundaries of society (Foucault 1980; Vermeersch 2005). However, I had to choose to accept the archive not as categorisation and labelling by the state but as an 'incomplete living institution' (Hall 2001). As a warning to the reader, in this chapter I do not rely on archival research, and whilst I draw on the research of other authors, notably on the extensive and influential work of Marushiakova and Popov, I write as an act of giving voice to something that has deeply influenced my own commitment to the study of Roma memory and has helped me to piece together a shared past through the stories of my informants. This chapter may only be a piece of an enormous historical puzzle, but its intention is to voice different narratives without contesting them and to provide an opportunity to historicise otherwise. The aim is to present life stories as the starting point and the exploration of life as lived to connect these stories of personal experience with their wider histories. Indeed, history, at least in part, can be understood and conceived through the small everyday acts of individuals and the histories that have brought them to their present place (Riessman 2008). Hence, I do not contest the historical value of the stories told by my informants; instead, I re-tell stories as 'an endless new chain of happenings whose eventual outcome the actor is utterly incapable of knowing or controlling beforehand' (Arendt 1977: 59).

This chapter is also about what my informants saw as the beginning of what it was and is to be Roma. In support of the core idea of the book, I present examples of the problematics of analysing Roma-ness through an anthropological lens and how the expression of historical Roma-ness can be a diverse expression of identities and representations (Buckler 2007; Marushiakova and Popov 2021). The unexpected elements here are found in the memories narrated in the stories that people shared with me and where one can find the individual reconstruction of life events as part of the public memory yet still not captured by mainstream history and archives. I rely heavily on life histories that have the capacity to draw out not only people's experiences but also the narrative strategies of remembering. Individual cases and narratives helped me to understand complex inter-relationships and how my informants related to the past (Riessman 2008). The past in people's imagination had multiple forms and consisted of numerous conflicting and complex versions. These narratives can also be considered as 'postmemory' (Hirsch 1997) to illustrate events for future generations.

A contextual and historical approach is necessary when accounting for how state politics impinged on Roma identification, particularly during socialism. I shall show that while the exclusion of Roma has been a constant trait throughout history, Roma have played roles in constructing Bulgarian identity and legitimating claims of Bulgarian 'culture'.[2] I engage with the particularities of the everyday negotiations of individuals who were and are often considered 'outsiders' within Bulgarian society. This chapter is, in a way, an attempt to add the principle of difference and heterogeneity to dominant historical imaginings of Bulgarian history in order to include alternatives to power-related memory politics. By presenting different historical narratives, I argue for what may be seen as unexpected or unusual narrations of positioning and belonging.

History and the State

As part of my research, I aimed to collect as many old photographs as possible as well as stories existing in the Radost Roma neighbourhood. I then asked people to share the stories depicted in the photos with me. The aim was that one day the pictures and stories would be presented in the Radost 'house of culture' (*chitalishte*)[3] and in the Radost history museum. The initiative was meant to inform people of the history of the Roma neighbourhood and to present a collection of images capturing different realities from those presented in the more popular historical accounts, which may see the creation of oral sources as biased or problematic.

The earliest historical evidence indicating the presence of Roma in the Balkans dates to the ninth century, and the first wave of large Roma settlements in Bulgaria can be traced to the twelfth (Marushiakova and Popov 2001). Large numbers of Roma also arrived in the Balkans during the Ottoman Empire in the fourteenth century, some of whom were sedentary and others who preserved their itinerant way of life and occupations well into the nineteenth century. Travelling was not necessarily always an economic choice for Roma, as illustrated in a conversation between Assuna (age 78) and her friend Rucha (age 75):

> Didn't our old people come from Drama? You know the lighter-skinned Roma women used to be called '*dramski tsiganki*' [the Gypsy women from Drama]. Around the time of the war [referring to the Balkan Wars in 1912 and 1913], my father and mother had to move from place to place, so they left Greece. They spoke in Greek and Romanes. Their cousins went to Turkey. My parents moved to Bulgaria, and so when I was young, people used to call me *dramska tsiganka*.

The newly established Balkan states did not recognise national minorities within their state borders, because this was conceived as causing harm to the nation-building process (Kitromilides 1989; Marushiakova and Popov 2001). In the Treaty of Lausanne of 1923, Turkey and Greece agreed on a major population exchange of two million people based on their religion. As part of the agreement, over one million Greek Christians and 500,000 Muslim Turks in the Anatolian and Greek lands were uprooted overnight (Kitromilides 1989). Muslim and Christian Roma in Drama (Greece), where Assuna's family resided, were part of this exchange. Some of them settled in Turkey, some were scattered throughout Greece and others settled in Bulgaria.

Nonetheless, travelling and geographical flexibility still played an important role in Roma socioeconomic life. Some traditional crafts, such as carpentry, basket weaving, ironmongery and blacksmithing required flexibility in location for economic survival. This was confirmed in my conversation with Assuna and Rucha:

In the old days, they moved from place to place. My grandfather used to tell us that he travelled with the King's army. He was proud that he fitted the shoes of King Boris' [referring to the Bulgarian King Boris III] horse. My grandfather was a well-known blacksmith. He taught my brothers also. When the communists began to rule, my family wasn't allowed to do these jobs anymore, so we all began working in cooperatives. My father still had his blacksmithing workshop, though. Nobody could stop him.

Prior to communism and under Ottoman rule, Roma were also involved in low-skilled work in the tobacco industry, in tin factories, as brick-layers (Ivancheva 2015) and as servants in large Bulgarian households, as in Rucha's parents' case. Figure 2.1 is the oldest photo in the Radost Roma neighbourhood. It depicts two Roma sisters and their children. One of the children is Rucha, who was aged three when the photo was taken. Rucha's father and mother were servants in a wealthy Bulgarian house-hold, and they took their children to work with them. She described how her mother and aunt dressed similarly to non-Roma women because they wanted to look 'clean and orderly, like the Bulgarians' and guarantee their acceptance and continuation of work in non-Roma households. They had to constantly negotiate and adapt to the dominant economic patterns to be self-sufficient.

Communism brought enormous changes to everyday life. The Bulgarian Fatherland Front[4] (*Otechestven Front*), 'the spearheading force of socialist construction', focused on efforts to create a socialist everyday culture (*sot-sialisticheski bit*) and promote the 'socialist way of life' (Brunnbauer 2008b). This way of life promoted 'proper life' and a new sense of community and opposed the bourgeois attitudes towards individualism (ibid). Socialism became 'doxa' (Bourdieu 1997), an inseparable part of everyday life, seen as 'natural' and part of embodied knowledge without any alternatives. The Fatherland Front defined what was not socialist by responding with rules and regulations. Despite the compulsory sedentarisation and geographical restrictions, Roma in Hungary, former Czechoslovakia and Russia found ways of moving by seeking locations where work matching their skills was available (Guy 2001; Lemon 2000; Okely 2011; Stewart 1997). Not for long, however. Roma transient way of life was 'un-socialist' and therefore Roma needed to join the proletariat, be emancipated and contribute to the anti-capitalist rebellion (Ivancheva 2015). Below is an excerpt from Decision #1360 of the Secretariat of the Central Committee of the Bulgarian Com-munist Party of 9 October 1978, summarising the rationale behind Roma sedentarisation:

The emphasis should be laid on their [Roma] involvement in labour which ben-efits society, on advancement in their education, on improvement in their living

Figure 2.1. The oldest photo – Rucha and her relatives. © Rucha Georgieva. Published with permission.

standards, on an increase in their consciousness and self-confidence as full-fledged citizens of socialist Bulgaria, on their growing participation in the building of a developed socialist society. (Marushiakova and Popov 1999: 68)

Roma had to become 'full-fledged' members or 'citizens' of the socialist society by shifting from 'unproductive people' viewed as the 'underclass'[5] to a social proletariat. Underclass as a label applies not only to those who stand outside of mainstream society and its central institutions but also to those who reject its underlying norms and values (Morris 1994). The morally different Roma were posing a challenge to the cohesion of the nation-state and its definition of citizenship. As a result, Roma became the object of exclusion and assimilation efforts in the name of inclusion, which aimed to erase cultural differences and turn them into industrial workers (Stewart 2001). The Communist Party aimed at providing waged labour to those who were looked upon as *lumpenproletariat* according to the prevailing Marxist ideology of the time (Ladányi and Szelényi 2001, 2003). Their 'vagrant way of life' involving 'crimes, begging and scavenging' had to change (Stewart 1997: 99). Their incorporation into the labour market was meant not only to eradicate Roma nomadism but also 'all aspects of Roma culture, without exception, were regarded negatively as relics from the past and as obstacles to their successful integration into wider society' (Guy 2001: 11).

The 'utopian' but also highly modernist ideology of communism, an intricate and not straightforward ideology with a definite underlayer of folklore, had to be applied to all spheres and social categories that affected Roma as well as other minorities. Initially, Roma were valued on the folk-loristic level but utterly excluded from the apparent modernist ideologies (Marushiakova and Popov 1999). For example, for a relatively short period of time (1945–1950), the leading political line was to promote Roma as an equal ethnic community within the Bulgarian nation and to encourage their active involvement in the construction of a new socialist society (ibid.). This is when the socialist regime aimed to support the culture, mother tongue and education of all ethnic communities, a policy similar to the '*korenizatsiia*' (indigenisation)[6] implemented earlier in the USSR (Marushiakova and Popov 2015; Oskanian 2021). Folkloric elements, such as ethnic music, dancing and dress, were now celebrated as expressions of culture and seen as the exotic element of the Soviet regime (Weitz 2002). Figure 2.2 illustrates how Roma in Radost were allowed to wear their traditional attire called *shalvari* (wide Turkish-style trousers with a short top) and to sing in Romanes. The figures depicts Roma women and men dancing in the centre of Radost on the 'Day of Culture'. Zuhra, one of my informants remembers:

> People liked us and enjoyed listening to and dancing to our music. I even remember the Leader of the Communist Party in Radost dancing with us. In time, though, we couldn't wear our *shalvari* anymore. We had to wear Bulgarian costumes, which we had to borrow from the 'house of culture'.

These somewhat flexible policies on cultural representation did not last long. The Party changed its tactic in the following decades. In its line of reasoning, the state had to take care of those groups who, because of capitalist exploitation in the past, were found to live in social and cultural 'backwardness'

Figure 2.2. Dancing in *shalvari* (1949). © Safka Kirilova. Published with permission.

(Marushiakova and Popov 1993, 1999). The Party had the ambitious goal to modernise and change the lives of these 'backward' groups by improving their levels of education and qualifications. Schooling was seen as the main path to socialisation, tasked with erasing any differences among children from different ethnic and religious communities and transforming them into 'builders' of the new socialist system (Hann 2002; Pelkmans 2009). Special classes for adult education were created for Roma, and education for all children became compulsory. Parents were punished for their children's truancy with fines or compulsory labour, and the share of Roma employed in the agricultural cooperatives, state-owned farms and industrial enterprises increased (Marushiakova and Popov 1993). Nelis (age 51) told me about the time she spent in the 'School of the Fatherland Front' in Assenovgrad, the first such school established in the country initially for women of ethnic minorities. This was a project directed at attracting young Roma, who were seen to be more active and 'well to do' in their respective communities. Nelis needed a recommendation from the Radost Leader (*Predsedatel*) of the municipality council in order to be accepted into the school.

> Our days were busy with learning how to cook, sew, read communist literature and, generally, how to behave. The teachers taught us good manners. The classes in communist ideology taught us about the role of the Communist Party and how it cared for the Bulgarian minorities. Everything we knew about the western countries had to be ignored. USSR was everything. We received certificates and went back home, where we were expected to become active volunteers in our communities. I organised sewing and cooking workshops for the women in the neighbourhood. I had to write a detailed report for the Radost's Fatherland Front Office and work with the *chitalishte* to encourage people, especially our women, to speak in Bulgarian and to send their children to school. The teachers would call the police if children from the neighbourhood didn't go to school. They contacted me first, and I had to report anyone who didn't go to school. Of course, I didn't report everything.

Targeting Roma women in communist education projects was of particular interest to the Party. Women as the main caregivers were going to influence their children in accordance with the communist ideology. The space for opposition and resistance was virtually non-existent during socialism, whereas political loyalty and adherence to the rules were rewarded with career prospects (Watson 1994). Nelis made sure that she followed the general rules; however, she also presented an 'evocative transcript', which anthropologists have explained as a way to present a different narrative in order to resist the repressive socialist regime (Humphrey 1994).

Although Roma labour participation increased, 'the attitude towards the Gypsies was not one of initial confrontation but rather an attitude adopted towards a community of a lower status whose members did not deserve special attention provided they knew their place and did not create problems' (Marushiakova and Popov 2005: 6). Roma labour, namely the bodily maintenance and assimilation into the proletariat, was widely accepted; however, Roma personage was a threat to the production of socialist society and had to be utterly rejected. Gradually, in the 1960s, Bulgaria adopted strategies of strict ethnic identity repression, involving the sedentarisation of Roma groups, closing down Roma newspapers and local community centres and banning the use of the Romani language (Marushiakova and Popov 2000).

The socialist governments of Eastern Europe aimed at extensive development and industrialisation, and these processes were implemented concurrently with Roma resettlements and compulsory sedentarisation. The centrality of the state, the production of its power and its effect on the representation of communities were focused on territory and the creation of spaces to embody the production of equal citizens, but often in reality in the case of Roma the state created segregation (Stewart 2001). The Party had some 'quick-fix solutions' (Ivancheva 2015: 49) to provide temporary settlements in response to the housing shortage across Bulgaria. Compact Roma settlements were 'hidden' behind tall concrete walls and became completely isolated pockets of peripherality (Stewart 2012). In Bulgaria, entire Roma settlements were demolished and replaced by urban buildings. Semi-legal housing and neighbourhoods consisting solely of Roma inhabitants burgeoned (Asenov 2018). Such was the case with Radost's Roma neighbourhood. The local Roma did not choose to live in this neighbourhood; the local authorities resettled them. Assuna's story presents some key aspects of the resettlement process. Assuna's father and grandfather who used to work for a wealthy Bulgarian man owned land and livestock. In time her father earned enough to build a house. He became the first Roma to own land and live amongst non-Roma in Radost. When the communist regime took over, the authorities confiscated all private land and took Assuna's father's property to build a hospital in the vicinity. In lieu, Assuna's family was given a plot of land on the outskirts of town, an area that merged with the industrial sector, where most of the previously itinerant Roma were settled. The new Roma quarter was called *Novodrumtsi* (Newcomers). Medo (age 68) also provided similar recollections:

> Our neighbours were not only Roma, but there were also Bulgarians. I don't know when my parents came to Radost. I only remember my grandmother and grandfather being servants for a local Bulgarian family. Why did we get to be moved from where we were to the end of town? I don't know. I only remember that there were a lot of us, and one house would have at least ten people living in it, and children were everywhere, roaming and playing. Maybe the Bulgarians got fed up with us.

My informants talked of how the *mahala* became home, and this space was undeniably interconnected with who they perceived themselves to be because space can be produced in economic terms and constructed in memories, images, social interactions and everyday life (Madanipour 2003). Its infrastructure, or lack of it, worked through the power of the state to implement policies and ideologies. The state, because of its territorial and ethnic boundaries, was threatened by the possibility of its disintegration and had to find ways to relocate, to re-space (Appadurai 1996; Foucault 1991). Opposing popular representations of Roma/Gypsies as wandering nomads, always moving and 'unsettled', the photos in this chapter also present a localised history, sedentarisation, a wish to settle and be situated, and a sense of belonging to the Roma neighbourhood. People recalled the oldest house in the Radost Roma neighbourhood and talked about the first radio and television. This was important for them because the house with the first radio became a community gathering place. They took pride in building new houses, settling, in having homes.

The resettlement occurred not only in spatial delineation but also in all aspects that would signify identification. The so called 'Process of Revival' took place in 1984–85 and was a policy specifically aimed at forcing Turks to change their Turko-Arab names to Slavic names (Marushiakova and Popov 2005). During this same period, the Turkish-speaking Roma had to change their names to Bulgarian names (Kyuchukov 2004). Assuna became Anastasia and Rucha was called Rumiana. All public documents were altered, and the designation 'Gypsy' (*tsiganin*) was omitted and changed to 'Bulgarian'. The category *tsiganin* (Gypsy) was no longer part of identity documents and official terminology. Along with banning the Romani language from being spoken in public places came the ban on wearing ethnic clothing such as *shalvari* as well as a ban on a widespread form of oriental dancing amongst Roma in Bulgaria called *kjuchek* (Silverman 1983). The *zurna*, an instrument played exclusively by Roma in the region, was prohibited in both private and public settings, since it was regarded as a Turkish or Muslim instrument (ibid.). Medo was a third generation *zurna* player and he told me:

> My great grandfathers played the zurna. One woman from the local museum told me that they have photos of my grandfather. We are well-known because we are four generations of zurna musicians. I know that for a long time, even when the Turks were in the land, we played music and entertained them. Then when the Party ruled, we continued to play our music secretly by gathering in areas where people wouldn't report us. I couldn't be only a zurna player, and I was also a worker in the local cooperative. I played the zurna on Saturdays and Sundays at our Roma weddings. Today, my children and grandchildren are all zurna players, and they are respected by all – Roma and non-Roma.

Along with the repression of all things Roma 'in culture', the state actively set out to create joint Bulgarian narratives through ceremonies and awards, which supported the spread of communist ideologies and aimed to erase ethnic, religious, class and cultural differences (Kaneff 2004). Roma had to appear like everyone else in all domains of life – music, dance,

Figure 2.3. House with the first radio (1953). © Medo Manev. Published with permission.

Figure 2.4. Building new houses. © Safka Kirilova. Published with permission.

attire, education and employment – while preserving, renegotiating and elaborating the social norms and customs of the surrounding population (Marushiakova and Popov 2015: 35–64). Despite representations of Roma and non-Roma as not sharing a history, in reality they occupied common spaces. The photos below illustrate the local dance ensemble, which by the late 1970s was one of the main initiatives of the Roma *chitalishte* in Radost. The *chitalishte*, which was a state as much as a community institution, and the Fatherland Front worked towards the active participation of all citizens (Kaneff 2004). The Roma of Radost wore Bulgarian traditional costumes and sang only in the Bulgarian language at performances. Rucha explained to me that speaking in Bulgarian, valuing the Bulgarian traditions and teaching these traditions to the younger generation was an important aspect of how well accepted Roma were by non-Roma.

Roma could not and did not run away from the state, as they struggled to be an integral part of it, including through education. Education became

Figure 2.5. Roma women dressed in traditional Bulgarian costumes. © Rucha Georgieva. Published with permission.

compulsory, and Roma children had to speak Bulgarian in public and in private. In the 1950s, the state commenced the building of schools for Roma in their secluded Roma neighbourhoods. The building of the first school in the Radost Roma neighbourhood was well received by the community, and it was seen as an exceptional achievement. Medo reminisced:

> The Party wanted our children to go somewhere when we were at work. Nobody was out of work, unlike today. I was about 12–13 years old when the municipality built a school for us. It was a small room on a hill, so it was visible from everywhere in the quarter. Only our children went to this school. At the time no one finished 4th grade. The little schoolroom was not enough for all the children, so they moved the school to a farmhouse with three main rooms, and they separated the children according to age. Our people helped build the school. My sons went to school there. We also got our first shop, and the shopkeeper was one of ours. We built the *chitalilshte*. We were doing well. The neighbourhood grew and grew.

Figure 2.6. Roma women and men performing in traditional Bulgarian costumes. © Rucha Georgieva. Published with permission.

The local 'house of culture' was built with space for a grocery store, a cinema and a kindergarten. The two-storey building was built one summer by Roma volunteers, and the locals took pride in the neighbourhood. The standard of living and Roma civil status improved during communism (Marushiakova and Popov 1993). Everyone had a job, access to free health care and mandatory education, and as Rucha told me:

> They [non-Roma] still overlooked us, but it was illegal to call us *tsigani* or bad words openly. We were supposed to be equal. We didn't worry about having enough to eat and about the education of our children. We had our own kindergarten in the 1970s in Radost. We didn't worry as much about the youngsters as we do now.

Radost also had its first female ambulance driver, who was a Roma woman called Isma. Her son Essat proudly showed me 'a piece of good history with a sad end'. Isma was the first Roma woman to graduate from high school, and her marriage was the first officially registered marriage of a Roma person in Radost. Isma died aged twenty-three from a severe haemorrhage after an illegal abortion. She was accused of having extramarital relationships with non-Roma men. Being a Roma woman who ventured into a male-dominated profession was too 'atypical' for the people in her community, as her son Essat told me. To be included, live by and adhere to the socialist rules, to

Figure 2.7. The new Roma kindergarten (1980s). © Maria Kamberova. Published with permission.

climb the social ladder, she risked estrangement from her community and her family. Still, Isma had a special place in the memories of the locals.

Despite the progress, the Communist Party's efforts to improve literacy, health and employment rates proved to be difficult and inconsistent. For example, although schooling increased under communism, many Roma children were sent to schools for children with learning difficulties. By the 1970s, such schools were officially called 'schools for children with inferior social status and culture' (Marushiakova and Popov 1999). In fact, many of these schools continued to function after the fall of communism (O'Nions 2010).

The collapse of communism in the late 1980s brought enormous changes to Central and Eastern Europe (Hann 2002; Kaneff 2011). This political and social upheaval had a profound effect on all members of the former socialist states. In November 1989, while there was a jubilee in Germany for the destruction of the most visible symbol of division between the Soviet Union and Western Europe, the Berlin Wall, the fear of the unknown gripped the Radost Roma neighbourhood. After years of assimilation efforts, suddenly Roma became openly 'the other' again. The process of reconstructing the socialist states began in accord with the emerging market economy and the neoliberalist ideology (Voiculescu 2019). This involved welfare state reduction, which pushed the most vulnerable in the population into extreme poverty and long-term unemployment. The economic crisis also brought enormous levels of open hostility towards Roma. Rada (age 59) remembers:

> The factories promised us that they will not make more than one member of a given family redundant. This promise was not kept for Roma. They lost their jobs in massive numbers because most of their jobs were in agriculture. In practice, what was happening to us was an economic genocide.

Anthropologists have described the survival strategies employed by households and individuals in postsocialist societies (Pine 1998, 2002; Verdery 1996). Radost Roma also devised strategies to survive, as Rada told me:

> Initially people had money, but there was nothing in the shops. Imagine queuing for hours just to get half a loaf of bread. This is when people began to travel to Macedonia and Turkey to buy goods and sell them back in Bulgaria. No one had a registered firm for trading or anything of that sort. People also earned their living from collecting scrap metal, picking herbs and recycling paper. Some of our Roma did this, but others got ill and passed away. We still haven't recovered.

Thirty years later, despite the many political and socioeconomic changes in Bulgaria, the legacies of socialism linger and can be found in state systems, in landscapes, in buildings, in memories – written and unwritten. It is important to understand the specifics of historical experiences to explain why, and how, they heralded a change in the role of the state and ultimately in the lives of its subjects.

Remembering and Forgetting

Social scientists have observed that the past, consisting of forced evictions, assimilations, inequality and discrimination, has forced Roma to constantly renegotiate identity in the present and has constructed their so-called 'indifference to' recollection (Lemon 2000). Several studies have documented that history and memory for Roma are constructed by choices they make in talking or not talking about the past. Roma have had a permanent representation as 'problematic citizens', 'stranger minorities', 'internal outsiders' (Bancroft 2001) and a 'menace' (Stewart 2012) who have chosen to live the way they do, facing poverty and exclusion, placing them as the marginal, foreign and deviant. These images are recycled constantly but have their roots in history and 'evidence the productive power of representation' (Gay y Blasco 2008: 301). The 'hunger to recycle' and repeat such representations is one reason not to portray Roma as populations who have a record of adjustment to social and political changes. In discussing the Gitanos' understandings of their own history, Gay y Blasco (2001: 631) suggests that ethnographers have missed opportunities to analyse Roma attitudes towards their origin or past and their alleged 'forgetting' or 'downplaying'. Such a tendency of 'communal forgetting' involves particular practices (e.g. information about past events and people is not passed on to the younger generations). Stewart (2004: 564) approaches the issue from a psychological perspective and contends that despite 'the Roma's presentist rhetoric', the past is remembered. He illustrates how the personal experiences of Roma during the Second World War have been remembered in time and turned into shared memories, despite the 'absence of commemorative ceremonies' and an 'obvious lack of interest' in re-creating their own history (ibid.). This process he calls 'living with the past' by 'remembering without commemoration'. Other authors also challenge the conception of Roma as a people 'who neither store and share memories of the past nor conceptualize themselves in terms of a desired future' (Kapralski 2013: 230).

As discussed in the previous chapter, Roma cannot be seen as a homogenous community or only as communities of shared social practices. However, just like other groups, Roma generate a collective identity or consciousness that is shaped by individual identities. The Bulgarian ethnographers Marushiakova and Popov propose that Roma in Eastern Europe exist at least in two dimensions, as a separate ethnic community and as an ethnically based integral part of society within the respective nation-state as citizens (2011). They further propose that the failure to consider the interlinked dimensional 'community/society' distinction can result in viewing Roma communities within the frames of being either marginalised or exoticised (ibid.). In the examples I present here, I continue this discussion and revoke critical thinking in binaries, categories and 'the absolute' by bringing to the forefront life histories that may render a more nuanced approach in considering Roma identification.

Even though oppression is an essential feature of Roma history, it is only a partial representation of Roma and their relations with non-Roma. In addition, the influence of political regimes, persecution, change, transition and life events such as weddings, births, deaths and others are narrated by my informants not only vis-à-vis the state and non-Roma but also vis-à-vis other members of the community and their kin. Authors propose that this process happens because of high demographic mobility whereby it is no longer necessary to remember ancestors left behind, but it becomes crucial instead to create new kinship (Connerton 2008: 63). Sometimes 'no memory is possible outside frameworks used by people living in society to determine and retrieve their recollections' (Halbwachs 1992: 43).

Moreover, the past is also about power and how power is maintained (Foucault 1980), kept secret (Carsten 2007) and controlled by the state and its mechanisms such as museums (Basu and Modest 2014), archives (Derrida 1996) and by historians, scholars and Roma themselves (Gay y Blasco 2001). Pierre Nora's concept for *lieux de mémoire* (sites of memory) conveys that memory is no longer a real part of everyday life and that these sites are 'embodiments of a commemorative consciousness that survives as a history' (Nora 1996: 6). Museums, archives, sites and other sources articulate the past, and this is how history with its record of the past has substituted the role of memory. Nora argues that memory, in opposition to history, evolves constantly and intersects with remembering and forgetting. Museums and monuments give embodiment to memories, and in a way they represent a more solid side of remembering; however, unwritten memories make us 'feel and think the past', hence we choose different ways to remember (Watson 1994: 8). Although there are few records pointing to the history of the localities and the people whom I researched, personal stories showed an interconnection with the local and national collective history. As opposed to views of Roma and non-Roma in mainstream historical accounts, especially the ones in museums and archives, as not sharing history with one another, the process of elicitation crystallised that they indeed shared and occupied common spaces and representations. Just as others did, the local Roma aspired to give their children the best start in life through education and employment, and they took part in celebrating local traditions and participated in everyday life. My informants also chose an array of strategies to remember, control, adhere to, forget, resist, talk about and suppress the past as is evidenced in the photos and the stories I uncovered.

Silencing and Forgetting

Considering the above approaches to Roma memory, I would like to provide glimpses of different ways of remembering. Some of my informants choose not to commemorate painful historical events, but their choices did not mean that these 'affective geographies' (Navaro-Yashin 2012), spaces, memories and stories were not remembered and passed down through rituals, songs, body movement and silence itself. Silence is often a very powerful vehicle for the transmission of unbearable memories. Often there is no need to commemorate or even articulate something that is always present and is happening now. The present encounters with violence, racism, removal and non-acceptance do not need a special place for memorisation. What is in the present cannot be forgotten. Remembering and forgetting then become selective acts of history-making because some histories can be 'unthinkable' (Trouillot 1995).

Some of my informants decided not to talk about the past, perhaps as a result of a decision to allow living space for present projects (Connerton

2008). Understandably, not everyone in Radost was eager to share their memories and photos with me. Jana, a Roma woman in her fifties, was most sceptical about the photo elicitation initiative. She was perplexed as to why I would ask about how people lived in the past and not be focused on how people were living now:

> You are asking too late. Most of our old people who would have known something about where we came from are not around anymore. Anyway, why do you have to know this? You will be better off not knowing. You are young and you have a future; why should you be interested in the past? Don't bring pain to yourself. Even if we had books about where we came from, who would care to read them? We are *tsigani*, and I can't think of anyone who would read about us. The Bulgarians cannot stand us, how would they read about us? Who are we? Anyway, if you write a book, write something good about us.

There was one definite pattern that I observed, and this was the internalisation of discrimination and exclusion. For Jana, this was too painful to recollect. She needed significant convincing and was surprised to hear that within Bulgaria and internationally, both in and outside academia, the history of Roma has been written about, debated and contested. The works of linguists, historians, folklorists, politicians, sociologists and anthropologists have attempted to shed light on Roma origins. When I explained to her that I was going to write a book and that this is why I wanted to record the stories and experiences of the people in the Roma neighbourhood, she responded:

> I know in the 50s or 60s we moved from another part of town, but this is all I know. If you are looking for something older, look at our skins. We are dark-skinned, and maybe India is our motherland. Actually, in 'The Law is Blind', a Hindi film from the 80s well known among Roma in Radost, I heard the word *pani* for water. This is our Romanes word for water too ... I don't know. Don't ask me. We don't really know where we came from. Why should I burden myself with thinking about pain?

Jana's experience of discrimination led her to believe that no one would be interested in reading about where Roma came from. Naturally, her experience of discrimination, or 'pain' as she called it, did not need further attention within the community and externally. Jana did not rely on a shared past with her contemporaries to have a sense of belonging to her community. The written or spoken record of history did not necessarily mean that the result was the collective preservation of identity. It was the shared sense of belonging in the present that Jana was emphasising. 'The old times' – that is, the past – was simply a period of forced assimilation, poverty and hardships that did not require voicing.

Obliterating

As I reviewed the collection of photos, I also came across specific patterns of controlling the past, meaning that some images were reshaped, reworked and cut out in order to hide past events and kinship relationships. By cutting out, scratching or destroying images, my informants negotiated the past vis-à-vis other community or family members. Sana (age 56) explained:

> We have many photos from weddings. We get married quickly and then separate, so the photos of previous marriages are destroyed, or people are simply cut out or scratched.

Talking about the past required talking about death, and this brought to the surface an array of emotions in my informants. Grief, sorrow, fear, pain and loss are experiences associated with death, and these feelings were often silenced. It was difficult for some of them to talk about their relatives who had passed away, and the silencing was apparent. Authors have written about the Roma/Gypsy attitude towards death and associated rituals (Okely 1983; Williams 2003). At times, Roma contain and then obliterate the recent past so that they are able to separate it from the present (Gay y Blasco 2001). The Radost Roma appeared to act similarly whereby they chose to talk or not talk about the dead and to erase memories by removing as many material reminders of people as possible, to control and resist the past. This is what Sana told me:

Figure 2.8. Cut out person as the couple is not married anymore. © Maria Kamberova. Published with permission.

Figure 2.9. Scratched faces – no longer in-laws. © Maria Kamberova. Published with permission.

We usually don't keep pictures of people who are dead. We don't want to disturb them. I shouldn't mention my mother's name, and I don't have photos of her when she was older. God forgive her, let her be in peace … Any possessions of the dead need to be destroyed – clothes and everything – together with their photographs. These are thrown into a river or burned. Maybe that's why our children do not know who their ancestors are.

From a first impression, it seemed that people did everything possible to erase the memory of the deceased and were reluctant to discuss loved ones. However, this seemingly 'neglectful' attitude on the surface had a deeper meaning. The beloved deceased were in fact treasured and protected through the burial rituals and afterwards in the mourning period and beyond. Sana did not need photos to remember her mother; she remembered 'deeper' in her own words. She did not want to speak about her in order to leave her deceased mother in peace. Sana also elaborately explained burial procedures, which required strict rules, including the disposal of the possessions of the deceased:

Every family has their own ways to bury the dead, but we have some common things we do as *tsigani*. The body has to be washed outside of the house, usually in the yard, and we put sheets around the place where the body is washed. The dead is put on a bed inside the house and covered in sheets. We don't leave the dead alone until she/he is buried. The keeping of the dead [the sitting up] continues throughout the night so that the relatives are not alone. People bring sweets, coffee and juice. From time to time, a relative will start to mourn out loud in a song to relieve their grief and to remember the deceased. In the night, all lights are on in the house of the dead and outside men light a fire and stay around it until sunrise. This is how other people learn if someone has passed away. Everyone is allowed to visit the home of the deceased. Even enemies can attend the funeral. Everyone is quiet and pays respect for the dead. The mourning period continues for forty days. Men don't shave, and women wear dark clothes and black scarves. They don't dance, and there are no celebrations.

Sana's detailed description is an example of elaborate mortuary rites of passage. Mortuary rites have many functions. Funeral customs remind the living that death and suffering are integral parts of nature (Douglas 1966; Huntington and Metcalf 1991). For Malinowski, death rites functioned to lessen anxiety. The crisis of death triggers 'a chaos of emotion', and the mortuary ritual dampens the potential danger to the individual and the group (Malinowski 1963: 97).

Resisting and Adjusting

As regards the past, alongside Bulgarian traditions, Roma secretly kept their own celebrations. The Roma of Radost knew how they were portrayed outside; they internalised these representations and acted upon them. The official assertion was that Roma had to adapt to changes and indeed during communism they largely did so. They also adapted in less popular and predictable ways. For example, despite the assimilationist efforts of the Communist Party, they continued to speak the Romani language at home and used their Muslim names inside kinship relationships. In fact, some of my older informants continued to be called by their Turkish names even by their non-Roma colleagues. At the end of the 1960s, all elements seen as Roma in attire, costumes, religious aspects, dance and music were replaced with the standards enforced by state institutions. However, in private settings, Roma musical forms thrived, and in Bulgaria the so-called 'wedding music', a musical genre largely represented by Roma, came to symbolise an anti-government resistance to state folklore (Silverman 2012). Roma had to have legally registered marriages and civil ceremonies, but Raba (Figure 2.10) was secretly wedded wearing Turkish Roma attire, in a ceremony that involved dancing to zurnas, despite the danger of being reported to the local Party leaders.

On the other hand, Daniela (Figure 2.11) remembers how she had to go outside the Roma neighbourhood and have a special civil marriage ceremony in the 'House of Culture' in Radost. The Party had created a pathway to follow, new authentic traditions to be shared by everyone – both Roma and non-Roma. More weddings became *komsomolski*, where only the closest relatives and friends of the newlyweds were invited. The latter were often not dressed in traditional costumes. No gifts were exchanged, and modesty was the motto of celebration. These types of weddings were held mainly in larger cities and were seen as more applicable to the educated Roma like Daniela who chose to keep 'in time with what was happening throughout the whole country – modernisation and future'.

Figure 2.10. 'Turkish Roma bride' (1960s). © Raba Ilieva. Published with permission.

Figure 2.11. 'New' socialist style wedding (1970s). © Rucha Georgieva. Published with permission.

To Conclude

For the purposes of this chapter, I located my thinking in the lifeworlds of my contemporaries, exploring their strategies to live their lives and to imagine, structure and fulfil them in the past and represent them in the present. It is the narratives such as those presented here that are behind the nowness of the everyday and offer not just some sense-making of the complex lives and identities of Roma but give us the chance to look at possibilities that are realised in the everyday. As I searched to find out histories and ways of remembering or forgetting, I was reminded that it is our experiences that make us who we are and determine how we create or choose not to create our life histories. Some of my informants chose to speak out and share their stories, and others did not see value in looking back. Thus, I do not pretend that presenting in-betweenness and ambiguity is a solution or the 'right way' to deal with the discussions on Roma memory. Instead, I advocate for further discussions and most of all for giving agency to the narrators – to forget or commemorate, to hide or display, to resist or give in, to follow traditions or not, and all in between, when it comes to the recollection of the past.

Just as my informants did, I connected the individual representations of social life, of the places where I lived and the people I met, with the wider collective historical representations. I argued that history, at least in part, can be understood and conceived of through the small everyday acts of individuals and the histories that have brought them to their present place. Asking why and how the local Roma in Radost explain, rationalise and make sense of their past offers insights into the social framework in which they operate and make choices but also how they manage the complex relationship between themselves, their kin and the state. Crucially, remembering and forgetting, downplaying and silencing memories are not only strategies concerning the past; they are about the present, which is constantly reminding of the past, and hence it is about the future also. This is a future of no past and present persecutions, assimilations and exclusion, one that Roma have and are hoping for, a time and space when they can be.

Regrettably, I was not able to organise an exhibition of the photo material presented here in the Radost museum, but I have not given up on pursuing this task in the future, including finding opportunities to screen the local archives. The local museum had only one relevant historical piece of evidence: a picture of the Roma *zurna* players, which my informant Medo showed me, and this image was presented as follows: 'Ethnographic aspects of a Bulgarian wedding'. Nevertheless, I am content that my informants still choose to remember, forget or create history in their own way. Perhaps this is their moral stance, to resist external identification or to have their say in determining who controls their past and present and who they want to be in the future. To become must begin from somewhere; it has a starting point because everyone starts somewhere, and Roma do too. For giving me the opportunity to present different histories, I am deeply grateful to the women and men who shared their stories and memories with me.

Notes

1. The Labor-Cooperative Farm (trudovo-kooperativno zemedelsko stopanstvo—TKZS) was established at the beginning of the communist rule in Bulgaria and closely resembled Soviet cooperatives in terms of organisation. It consisted of state-controlled farming based on land taken from private landowners in the pre-Second World War era (Kaneff and Leonard 2002).
2. The critique of the concept of 'culture' entails a shift from coherent and homogeneous cultures towards analysis of fragmentation, contradictions and multiplicity (Appadurai 1996; Hannerz 1992).
3. *Chitalishte* translated in Bulgarian literally means 'a place to read'. The *chitalishte* was established mainly as a voluntary educational institution to promote democracy and national identity (Valkov 2009: 428). Authors argue that the creation of the *chitalishte* was an idea influenced by Western Europe, dating back to the Ottoman rule of Bulgaria, and its main purpose was to 'transfer education to the masses' (ibid.). While in other countries (Britain, France, Germany, Serbia, Albania and Turkey) similar concepts to *chitalishte* were not preserved, in Bulgaria the idea became a mechanism for national identity and belonging (ibid.: 429). Later, Stalin's Russia developed a network of the so-called 'houses of culture', which focused on 'culture' as folklore (Donahoe and Habeck 2011). This influenced other socialist countries, where the 'houses of culture' functioned under the Soviet framework. Other authors hypothesise that the Soviet 'house of culture' system was tailored after the already existing Bulgarian network of *chitalishte* (Savova 2007). The Soviet 'house of culture' also hosted predominantly professional performances, whereas the *chitalishte* remained a place for amateur creativity (ibid.). Today, Bulgaria keeps a nationwide state-funded network of community cultural centres (mostly still called *chitalishte*) in almost every populated area of the country (ibid.).
4. The Fatherland Front aimed at creating the 'New Man' and the 'socialist way of life'. It was envisaged to provide social involvement for non-Communist Party members, 'where people would come together on the various fronts of socialist construction and would internalize the norms and values of socialist community' (Brunnbauer 2008: 45).
5. For Ladányi et al. (2001, 2006), Roma in communist times moved through 'cyclical phases': from lower class to under-caste and underclass. Morris (1994) in her book *Dangerous Classes* points out that disentangling what 'underclass' means is complicated because of the looseness of the definition.

6. 'Indigenisation' in Russia promoted national languages and culture through various national institutions, including schooling (Liber 1991). This process of indigenisation involved voluntary resettlements and the emphasis on and promotion of folklore.

CHAPTER 3

EDUCATING ROMA CHILDREN
State and Kinship Moralities

I explained my research to Mrs Stoyanova, a head teacher, in a phone conversation prior to our meeting in person; however, it never occurred to me to introduce myself as a Roma researcher. It was during our in-person interview that I realised my researcher identity did not entirely fit within Mrs Stoyanova's perceptions of Roma. Once I mentioned that I was living in Radost's Roma neighbourhood and that I grew up in a Roma neighbourhood elsewhere in Bulgaria, Mrs Stoyanova paused and said 'Well, you must be an exception!' Our conversation came to an end quickly afterwards.

In this chapter, I set out to illustrate the conflict and contradiction between different regimes of morality (Berliner et al. 2016; Robbins 2016), and I explore some of the tensions arising from historical and current relationships between Roma and the state and how these relationships have evolved more specifically, drawing from the realm of education. There are tensions between different actors, between domains – private and political, kinship and polity – and between ideologies and power relations. Crucially, what is apparent in the situations I describe is that a particular individual's attitude towards education is based on their values; values that may seem wrong and immoral to another. Thus, I present snapshots of the multilayered and often contradictory experience of marginality whilst exploring the highly individualised, subjective and circumstantial nature of identification.

While I present a complex picture, I request the reader to bear with me as I endeavour to translate multiple perspectives regarding Roma education. Roma experience their place in society as on the axis of community and the state, and I focus on the contradictions inherent in this. My warning to the reader is that the empirical strength of this chapter is in the narratives of my interlocutors, of their dilemmas, hopes and desires. There are various aspirations, moralities, understandings, hierarchies and inequalities. I introduce many actors, stories and narratives, and I do so in line with the arguments put forward by this book; namely, to illustrate the contradictions between different actors, such as teachers, parents, children, state officials, as well as between domains – public and private – producing both exclusion and inclusion. What I convey here is an imperfect situation and dis-synchronisation both within schools and within the community. The contradictions in ideologies affect power relations, and I argue that there is a clash of moralities as I look at how Roma education is perceived by teachers, state representatives or 'outside' actors and how education is reproduced and confronted 'inside' kinship relationships.

Conventionally, much attention has been paid to tangible ways of supporting Roma children in schools, through curricula inculcating certain values, which I write about in emic terms as moralities instilled through instruction and training, but less attention is focused on what happens inside their homes and communities. In addition to the more mainstream analysis of the dichotomy between state and community, I also consider the divisions and fragmentation within the state and the kin or community. Most importantly to me, I provide partial glimpses of children's sense of belonging, their aspirations and how they navigate the different realms of school and home.[1]

The Teachers

Although often referred to as an 'unemotional structure', the state is constituted by physical persons who act on the basis of emotions, 'values and affects' when it comes to the practical execution of policies (Fassin 2015). These state actors have different moral proclivities and positions that range from rigid interpretation of policies to a more flexible and partial commitment towards their implementation. Value subjectivities are then displayed by the supposedly impartial state system. In what follows, I provide the narratives of three teachers to illustrate how they interpret state policies and conceive of their work as educators to Roma children. The state has powers to enforce specific requirements for education, but self and state can be combined – social and political interventions can be implemented by state agents who reinforce state moralities as they deem fit. In practice, schools can reinforce the 'otherness' of Roma children, despite education being seen as the most important aspect of Roma inclusion (Van Baar 2011; Vermeersch 2006). What is common in the narratives that follow is that social policies regarding education view Roma children only through the prism of citizenship in order to produce adequate adult citizens with the ability to self-govern (Gay y Blasco 2016). Yet, education participation rates among

Roma children are lower as compared to main populations not only in Bulgaria but across Europe.

Mrs Stoyanova

Neli, whose family I lived with in Radost, was working on a project that aimed to connect Roma parents, most of them mothers, with the governors of the local schools to establish an interethnic dialogue and participation in the educational life of the town. Neli introduced me to Mrs Stoyanova. She was the long-term head teacher of the local Gymnasium (High School), the best performing school in Radost, with a hundred-year history. Only 3 Roma children out of 185 were studying at the Gymnasium. In Mrs Stoyanova's words, this was partly because the school was located far from the Roma neighbourhood and children had to walk a long distance, and partly because the school was providing education to the local *crème de la crème* population, a social layer in which Roma parents were not categorised. Mrs Stoyanova was proud of her school's reputation, which she guarded fiercely and maintained by not accepting pupils whose circumstances would change the excellent results and dynamics of her school. Many of the children who graduated from the Gymnasium went on to become doctors, engineers and teachers, and Mrs Stoyanova proudly kept pictures of such role models on the walls of her office. First, she assured me that Roma children and their parents are treated equally in her school, regardless of their ethnicity and then she went on to tell me how two of the Roma children in the school were not regular attendants and struggled with achieving good results, so only one of them was an *otlichnichka* (excellent student). Mrs Stoyanova revealed that her long career of over thirty years in education had taught her to recognise which children were going to excel at school and which were going to fail.

Today, a common practice for some teachers is to have a respectful attitude towards some students and a deliberately negative one towards others. I understand this and would like to explain it. We have hidden expectations regarding the potential of different pupils. That is, if a teacher believes that a child has a high success rate they will do well. The opposite is also true. Some children, such as Roma children, may need more support at school, and a fraction of them can do better. However, I have been around for a long enough time to be able to predict who will do well and who will not. Most Bulgarian children are honest, cultured, ambitious, curious and intelligent. They are also less aggressive. As a young teacher, I taught many Pomak[2] children, so I know that there is a difference. They were disciplined and had a lot of respect for the teachers. They were very modest, quiet and some of the children did well. The Roma children, on the other hand, are stronger physically, they are beautiful children, but many do not do well intellectually because they lack discipline. They usually display aggression. This is because their parents are not interested in their children's education; it is their home environment, and this is who they are. It is irresponsible in my opinion. They use their children for everything and anything to earn money, and they do not see education as a priority ... they marry them off early in lavish celebrations but say that they cannot afford to buy them clothes to come to school.

Mrs Stoyanova's observation about teachers systematically misinterpreting children's 'cultural capital' (Bourdieu 1997) was disappointingly accurate. Bourdieu's concept of 'cultural capital' illustrates how educational credentials help to reproduce and legitimate social inequalities, as higher-class individuals are seen to 'deserve' their place in the social structure more than others. In other words, educational success can be largely predetermined. As children from different social backgrounds become more selected, they progress through the education system differently. The children in Mrs Stoyanova's school who had 'cultured' competencies were selected within an educational system that was designed to recognise and reward children who were 'honest, cultured and ambitious'. These qualities were not ascribed to Roma children, whose culture was 'backwards', 'naturally inferior' and in desperate need of the 'dominant' naturalised culture. This logic puts at an advantage the children who possess the values and the morality of the dominant group but discredits those children who supposedly lack the morality, citizenship and obedience of the former group. Ultimately, it is parents who are to blame for not placing enough value on education and discipline. Fortunately, not all teachers in Radost shared Mrs Stoyanova's views.

Mr Janakiev

Mr Janakiev introduced himself as 'a committed to egalitarianism professional who loves history'. Close to half of the pupils attending Mr Janakiev's school were Roma children. His school was also part of Neli's project and had a well-established parent participation group as part of the governance of the school, with Roma parents as members. The most recent attempts of the Bulgarian state authorities to return Roma children to school had proved successful in Mr Janakiev's school. In his words, 'for the first time since the fall of communism, Bulgaria has small armies of teachers, social workers and police officers who work for the inclusion of Roma children at school.' In the last couple of years, the school had seen an increase in Roma pupil attendance and better education results. He also had plans to organise more after-school activities, days of art and culture and home visiting. His ideas, however, needed additional school resources. Mr Janakiev used to be the deputy mayor of Radost, with responsibilities including the disbursement of educational resources for the municipality. The local government did not typically demonstrate enthusiasm towards securing Roma or minority education funding, even when funding existed within national Roma education programmes. Mr Janakiev was of the opinion that the local authorities either lacked the initiative to apply for national funding or sought to divert the funding towards other less controversial causes.

> It is hard to convince my colleagues that we need to support those children who come from underprivileged backgrounds. However, the local governors cannot afford to invest in the minority population because this is not going to win them the mainstream electoral vote. There is only one aspect with which the local authorities are concerned, and this is the high Roma birth rate. The national government as well as the local authorities face a problem – a large share of the young Roma population who have lower levels of education and are deemed incapable of contributing to the county's economy.

Mr Janakiev was frustrated as his previous colleagues often discussed how the state system, including schools and social and health services, was going to be 'overloaded' by Roma demand. The rise in the Roma population, however, was a 'problem' with a double solution – ignore demands for further investment in the community and focus on cutting access to any existing benefits. Frustrated by the misjudgement of the local authority at the end of his political term, Mr Janakiev decided to go back to his role as a school principal. He aspired to show a different kind of school to the local authorities and beyond; however, it was the very system he worked in that prevented him from doing so.

> It is no secret that school directors refuse to accept Roma children in their schools because of the fear that the Bulgarian children will leave. Only recently one mother threatened to move her child to a different school since more than half of the children in my school are Roma. The mother complained to the mayor's office, and the school is now being pressed to stop accepting more Roma children.

Mrs Manova

Mrs Manova was a teacher in Mr Janakiev's school. She was convinced that working with pupils outside formal education in a way that brought education to their homes was most beneficial for them. Mrs Manova believed that the school was not a 'tabula rasa' system where teachers were responsible for a student's entire body of knowledge. She thought, as Freire did (Freire 1972), that it is not the intellectual elite, the dominant group, who produce those moments of change for 'the oppressed' but the power of the individual that will initiate the process of transformation.

Helping Mrs Manova with her afternoon classes became one of my main activities during my stay in Radost. Mrs Manova had undertaken the role of visiting families and children at home once a week on her own initiative. Also, in collaboration with the Roma evangelical church she organised parent meetings and after-school activities to help children with their homework. At the time, the government had introduced incentives for teachers of minority pupils while implementing measures to stop social payments for parents who refused to send their children to school. The school attendance in Radost increased; however teachers were passing pupils from one school year to the next without there being any real improvement in their grades. Mrs Manova, who knew the children and the parents well, explained:

> You can put all your efforts into reaching the children, but if their parents don't have money for clothes and food, there is no point. My fellow teachers will only continue to give them the minimum marks to pass, and there will be no real improvement. At times, what we teach at school doesn't fit with what children experience at home. We put Roma parents in that difficult position where they need to compete with the system in order to provide what we think is best for their children. Also, often they may not have the opportunity to provide for their children because of a complex set of issues such as unemployment, lack of service support, health and even something as simple as not having food to put on the table. I am astonished that many of my colleagues know very little about how Roma children walk through roads full of mud for nearly 3 km each way to get to school. This is what I call parental commitment.

Through the three examples of teacher narratives, I illustrated how the physical persons representing the state act on the basis of emotions, moralities, impartialities, preconceptions and values (Fassin 2015). Apparent is the different interpretation of educational policy implementation and the divisions between state actors. Mrs Stoyanova understood her role as a guardian of her school's reputation and therefore in not allowing the acceptance of Roma children she was protecting the quality of her school environment at the expense of the non-dominant social group. Mr Janakiev had professional goals of showcasing his school as the best example of an inclusive model, and although he understood the context in which Roma children lived, he was faced with hindrances posed by the local administration, the very state domain that was supposed to encourage him to pursue his ambitions. Mrs Manova took matters outside the school walls and went into the Roma neighbourhood to support her pupils. Her involvement was not unproblematic; she did not have the approval of relatives and friends.

The Parents

As indicated earlier in the chapter, socio-structural explanations for barriers that inhibit the achievement of Roma children have resulted in different conclusions concerning 'Roma culture' and its morality. Some explanations locate poor performance and deviant behaviour within a cultural deficit, oppositional culture, or culture of poverty and 'underclass' models (Ladányi and Szelényi 2006). Other studies present how education is viewed inside the community; most often as alien (Daskalaki 2004; Engebrigtsen 2015). Here I present fragmented parental responses to education that provide a clue as to the imperfect fuzzy, non-identical nature of relationships 'inside' the kin and the community. In Radost, Roma children, parents and grandparents often live together or at least close to each other. Child-rearing is the responsibility of everyone in the family, and teenagers are expected to begin adult socialisation, including helping their parents and relatives, from an early age. Family is a priority, and children learn this from an early age.

Mila

I joined Mila as she prepared her daughter Silvia for her first day in Mrs Stoyanova's school. Mila was excited that her daughter was starting school. She bought beautiful fresh flowers the day before, and as she ironed Silvia's brand-new clothes, she told me about her own childhood:

> I came from nowhere. My family didn't have anything while we grew up. My mother and father were growing tobacco and peanuts, so my two sisters and I joined them in the fields from an early age. My parents wanted us to study but life was hard. We were villagers so sending us to high school in Radost wasn't an option. Also, you know by the time I was fifteen I was going out with Mitko, and we got married soon after. Studying was out of the question. Today I want a better life for my Silvia.

Silvia's father, grandmother, grandfather and aunty were waiting outside in front of the gate, dressed in their best attire for the occasion. 'You must study unlike your grandpa and grandma' – said Silvia's grandfather. 'Be blessed my dear child, in all you do' – said her grandma. The aunty, after whom Silvia was named, was a high school teacher in a nearby city. She embraced her niece and said 'You will study in the best school, and one day you will replace aunty as a teacher in her school. Agreed?' Silvia nodded enthusiastically, and as they walked to the centre of the town through the neighbourhood, people on their left and right were wishing Silvia and her family well.

A month after Silvia's first day at school, Mila called Neli and me to tell us about her experience dealing with the Gymnasium. Silvia was bullied by another pupil who did not want to sit next to her because she was a *tsiganka*. Mila was disappointed. She talked to the class teacher, who eventually moved Silvia to the desk at the end of the classroom to sit on her own. Silvia was the only Roma child in her class, and she came home upset that there was no one to play with her.

Mila faced a dilemma, a decision that Roma parents face daily – to send her child to experience discrimination at school or shield her at home. Mila had taken a loan to pay for Silvia's uniform and school materials. Even though she considered education important for her child, she also saw such expenses as an obstacle. Primary education in Bulgaria is officially free of charge, but costs such as the purchase of clothes, books or any additional expenses must be covered by the parents. The school represented a hostile environment, a place where children experienced prejudice, and it became a mechanism that reproduced inequality (Daskalaki 2004). Eventually, Mila ended up transferring Silvia to Mr Janakiev's school.

Emi

Various stereotypes were utilised, acted on, and even incorporated into the school curriculum. Emi, the mother of 9-year-old Snezhana, showed me pictures from a Bulgarian textbook showing a Roma woman as the 'ugly, bad liar'. The textbook featured a well-known Bulgarian fairy tale called 'The Unborn Maiden', written by the writer Ran Bosilek. The prince in the tale ends up marrying the bad, black and ugly Gypsy woman who lies to the beautiful and naïve white and golden maiden with whom the prince is in love. The *tsiganka* in the story does this in order to take the maiden's place in the prince's palace. The story is about rejecting everything deemed 'Gypsy' as bad and ugly. The main text is followed by a task to match the qualities of the main characters – the maiden – clever, trusting and beautiful – and the *tsiganka* – bad, jealous and lying.

This identity-based discrimination and differing moralities trickled through the provision of education (Dunajeva 2014). Snezhana came back home and asked her parents why they were called *tsigani* and told them that she did not like her brown skin, as it looked like the skin colour of the *tsiganka* in her textbook. She 'knew how to read and count', so Emi decided to stop her from attending school. The school had presented Snezhana with practical knowledge, and she was able to start helping her mother in her little shop selling sweets. In theory and in practice, education was supposed to allow children to develop into autonomous adults to be able to function in society on an equal basis with everyone else.

Rumi

I met Rumi, the mother of a 4-year-old girl, at the central playground in Radost. She was disappointed that her daughter was not accepted by one of the town's mainstream kindergartens.

> For decades there has been discrimination in the education system in Radost. It all started in a kindergarten that was designed to accept only Roma children. This doesn't bother some Roma parents, because they silently resign to what is being said about them. I want my children to have a better future. I would like them to have the same chances for education as the Bulgarian children.

When Rumi wanted to meet with the director of what was known as the best kindergarten in town, which the locals referred to as 'the Palace', it was difficult to arrange a meeting. The teachers told her that there were no more available places, but she kept asking for a meeting with the director, who eventually met with her and told her to take her daughter to the Roma kindergarten. Rumi felt as if she was 'a second-hand human' ('*chovek vtoro kachestvo*'), but she did not give up. She asked Neli and me to help her write a letter to the mayor and the municipal council. Following this, the director of the kindergarten was asked 'to compromise' and accept Rumi's daughter into her kindergarten.

Krassimira

Krassimira was spending every afternoon helping her two children, one aged 11 and the other 17. She worked as a cleaner in a local hotel and made arrangements to be at home every afternoon before she went back to work in the evening. She was particularly determined to help her 17-year-old daughter get into university and wanted to save as much money as possible to be able to support her even though her family struggled financially. Krassimira's husband was doing seasonal work abroad, and he was not able to save enough money to send back home.

> It is very hard to be a Roma mother. For example, if our children are sick usually this is the responsibility of the mother. It is different for the Bulgarian parents; they both go to the hospital when their children are sick, or when there are parents' meetings in school, or when parents need to help each other. I go to the parents' meetings on my own and that is if I can escape from work. If I don't attend these meetings, the teachers say that I am an irresponsible parent, and they tell my children off.

Krassimira would give everything to see her children finish school. The best advice she had for her daughter was to keep away from boys while she was studying because this would save her from an early marriage and from repeating her mother's struggles.

Nevena

It was a warm summer evening and Nevena's husband was sitting in front of the house, drinking beer together with the neighbours. I asked whether his wife was at home, and he pointed me to their backyard. In an almost apologetic voice, Nevena's husband told me that he had stopped his daughter Mirka, aged sixteen, from attending school. 'This school business is no good. She can stay at home and help us.' Nevena's husband did not disclose more details but willed me to see his wife, as if there was more to the story that she could explain. Nevena was sitting in the garden with her sister-in-law and one of the neighbours. I understood that one day on Mirka's way to school a car pulled right in front of her and made her get in. 'This silly boy from that village wanted to marry Mirka, so he decided to abduct her. I tell you, the anger and the rage we felt when we learned about this. Awful!' – said Nevena. A man from the neighbourhood saw this and called Mirka's father, so he and his sons jumped in the car and went straight to the boy's house and took her back home. In answer to my question about whether they had called the police, Nevena looked at me in disbelief. 'Are you crazy? How would you call the police? What if the boy slept with her? How would we carry that shame with us?' To prevent people from talking about Mirka's honour, Mirka's parents stopped her from going to school. Mirka was heavily guarded by everyone and most of all by her two brothers, who were ready to fight any young man who dared to approach her. Mirka's honour had become even a matter of protection by the neighbours. 'I know you like schools and things, but Mirka needs to stay home. Her parents are doing the right thing' – the neighbour told me. Interestingly, I had not expressed preference or support towards either going to school or not.

Mirka and her parents received a call from her class teacher, who mentioned how well Mirka was doing at school and that it was a pity to prevent her from getting an education. The parents kept repeating that Mirka did not need to study any more, since she was going to help with the family business. There were two different understandings, values and morals at work: the parents thought they were saving Mirka's future, and the teacher thought that they were destroying it. Leaving school early was ethnicised and attributed to Roma culture and poverty without consideration of the history of the practice and its appropriation from a wider social context. Anything, including marriage, preventing schooling was morally wrong (Cupelin 2017; Kovai 2011; Tesar 2012). It was easier for Mirka's parents to accept the moral stance of the school and to quietly resist it than having to explain the details of why Mirka needed to stay at home in accordance with the communal understanding. This was summarised by Nevena like this: 'Mirka's teacher will never understand that honour is more important than school. One day Mirka's husband will not look at her diploma and congratulate her on her good marks. He will treat her well if she is honourable.'

Externally, the parents appeared relieved because they had managed to 'prevent the worst' and to protect Mirka from becoming 'dishonourable' (meaning not being a virgin). In private, however, the situation was more complex. Both parents were divided and struggled with the choice they made. Mirka's mother had plans for her daughter. She thought that Mirka would become a lawyer one day, and earlier in our meetings she shared how she would have moved to wherever Mirka went to study to support her. Mirka's mother searched for my approval:

> I know you would understand me, Iliana. Who would let their daughter go to school after what happened? The people in the neighbourhood are talking already that she is not honourable. Nothing happened to put this shame on my child's head and our family. Who would marry her if I let her go back to school? We are not like the Bulgarians whose daughters can do whatever they like; they go to school freely, they get educated, have good jobs, and marry men whom they want to be with.

Finding a husband, being married and being part of a kindred group was more important than what school was going to give Mirka, and they could not imagine a rupture with what was expected of them. This is what Herzfeld calls 'cultural intimacy' – that is, 'the recognition of those aspects of a cultural identity that are considered a source of external embarrassment but that nevertheless provide insiders with their assurance of common sociality' (Herzfeld 2014: 3). A few months later, Mirka married the boy who had allegedly abducted her, and I was invited to her wedding. Marriage and honour were paramount, and in Chapter 6 I provide more details as to why.

In this section, I gave examples of Roma parents, their individual circumstances and their experiences of education as reproduced and confronted by the state as well as by kin. In the narratives, the state isolates, perpetuates and enforces its dominant 'culture', and there are few attempts to understand the internal struggles faced by Roma parents. The parents were painfully aware of the discrimination faced by their young children. Mila made the choice to move her daughter to a different school, and Emi decided to shield her daughter at home. Rumi wanted her child to get used to being in the 'outside' world of a mainstream kindergarten from an early age, which she believed would guarantee more acceptance and better education results as her daughter grew up. Krassimira struggled financially, but she was ready to support her children in education at any price. Nevena faced what the community perceived as the 'unthinkable' and had to sacrifice her daughter's education so that she could be respected by the community. Often the role of the 'informal', the kin perceptions of education, are seen as the opposite of state education. This competition between the home and the school/ the state – to bring up Roma children with appropriate values, morality and control – creates at times two impossible worlds for Roma children.

The Children

Here, I focus on life and education 'inside' the Roma family and neighbourhood from the perspective of children. I look at adulthood as corresponding with childhood as a social category within chronological time (James, Jenks and Prout 1998), fixed and translated through social practices inside the Roma kin, neighbourhood and domain as opposed to the state practices outside the community. Conclusively, this framework shows that the 'child' as a social category in the Roma and non-Roma contexts is in many ways arbitrary because notions of what it is to be 'a child' vary within and between cultures, over time and across generations (James and James 2004). The popular understanding is that childhood is a critical period for preparing children for their future roles as adults, but this discourse considers children only in terms of their future becoming, rather than being 'somebody' in their own right (James, Jenks and Prout 1998). Moreover, discourses about Roma children in the social sciences and in policies tend to view them as 'innocent victims' with endangered futures, children who are at risk from 'irresponsible' Roma parents or discriminating school institutions and teachers. From the stories I present here, it becomes clear that the cultural and social agency of Roma children can determine their school performance and success levels. In the process of talking to children, I saw them as active participants whose perspectives were not only important in their own right but whose accounts are taken as competent portrayals of valid experiences (Thelen and Haukanes 2010).

Snezhana (9 years old)

Snezhana, Emi's daughter, whom I referred to earlier in the chapter, did well in her education but eventually was stopped from attending school. She was the child that noticed how the *tsiganka* is portrayed in 'The Unborn Maiden' fairy tale. At age nine, Snezhana was helping her single mother with cleaning, cooking and looking after her brothers at home. This was our conversation:

Iliana: What is a child Snezhana?

Snezhana: You must be good, to go to school, to help … You know I go to school with Marko [younger brother] and he is only little, so I fight with the children who hit him at school. Marko is a child.

Iliana: Why do they hit him?

Snezhana: They call him dirty *tsiganin* (Gypsy) and then hit him, but I then hit them back.

Iliana: What does Mom say about this? (Emi looks upset as she hasn't heard this story before).

Snezhana: I don't know. I don't like school anyway.

Iliana: Mum knows now. Maybe she can help?

Snezhana: She is *tsiganka*. They will not like her at school too.

Snezhana understood that family was above everything else. She not only protected her brother at school, but she also spared her mother from the details of knowing what her children were experiencing. Her moral stance was centred on the protection of her family. She knew how she was perceived and that the presence of her mother at school was not going to help. Snezhana acted autonomously to defend her brother, despite being seen as aggressive at school, and wanted to protect her mother from being exposed to discrimination. She also understood what the school expected of her as a Roma child, how she was perceived by this 'outside' world, and she acted according to these expectations. The 'informal' – home and kinship – relationships, the cleaning, the care for her brother, and helping in her mother's sweet shop were the unknown activities in the 'external' world of state education. In reality, Snezhana was the epitome of what is seen to be a 'good' child inside the community, as her help was invaluable to her single mother. Ironically, the 'outside' world did not seem to be interested in Snezhana's domestic experience, yet both domains (state and kin) in their own way aimed to produce 'good children'. In this sense, the state and the home were producing the same outcome – the reproduction of a 'good' self.

Iskra (7 years old)

Iskra had just started school in Mr Janakiev's school. Her class teacher was concerned that Iskra's strong accent in the Bulgarian language was becoming problematic at school. Children laughed at her, and she began to withdraw from participating in class. Her peers were also calling her 'the *tsiganka* who cannot speak'. Iskra's parents spoke to her mainly in Romanes and Turkish at home, and Neli asked me to help by reading and talking to Iskra in Bulgarian. I spent a couple of afternoons with her when she found the courage to ask me: 'Where is your mother?' I explained that she was at home and that I was in Radost because I wanted to learn and write a book about children like her.

She laughed, 'A book? Only teachers write books.' Apart from the Bible in the corner of a cupboard, there were no other books in Iskra's home. Iskra's parents had acquired the Bible in church, where Neli and Mrs Manova were providing literacy classes to adults. 'Are you a teacher also?' Iskra asked me. I told her that I was not but that perhaps she would like to be a teacher one day. 'No, I want to be like mama. I want to feed my baby ...' she replied. Her mother interrupted her 'You want to be nobody like me' and then she turned to me: 'School is good, but I don't want her to be upset by the Bulgarians. As long as she can count and read, I will be happy.' Iskra did progress with her spoken Bulgarian in the next couple of months, but her peers contin-ued to call her 'the *tsiganka* that cannot speak'. It had not occurred to her school, or perhaps it did not matter, that at age seven Iskra spoke three lan-guages (Turkish, Romanes and Bulgarian), which was more than most of the children in Radost spoke. Her Romanes and Turkish language acquisition belonged to the private, 'internal', nonstate realm. Kinship had its limitations (Pine 2018: 100), and the mother tongue mattered only in the undervalued domestic circumstances.

Nikol (11 years old)

Nikol was 11 years old when I met her. She was *otlichnichka* (an excellent student) in Mrs Stoyanova's *Gymnasium*. Her class teacher was supportive of Nikol's progress and thought that she was highly unusual in her pursuit of learning and enjoying all school subjects. Nikol's mother and father never finished primary school. Lena, Nikol's mother, was humble about her child's excellent school record. 'It is always difficult to find the money for clothes, for books, for breakfast ... but we do what we can. It is up to Nikol to decide whether she studies or not. I can't help her with her homework. She does it herself.' Nikol had three older siblings, who left school early. At home, there was no pressure on her to do well education-wise, but at school, she had to compete with the requirements of the education system. How she negoti-ated both worlds was by performing differently in each of them. She told me that at school she imagined that she was not a *tsiganka,* and the moment she left the school gates she was Roma again. She had become 'the unusual' student in Mrs Stoyanova's school. What her teachers did not know was that Nikol had her parents' complete trust and autonomy to choose whether to study or not. She dreamed of becoming a doctor so that she could help her sick grandmother. To achieve her dream, she had to experience, express, manage and perform her identity differently and according to context. Nikol's independence was commendable, and although she did very well at school, I doubt her peers and teachers knew how challenging it was for her to navigate the two different worlds of family and school.

Stefan (12 years old)

Stefan was not keen on going to school. Although he was receiving support from Mrs Manova, he was lagging behind other pupils. His absences from school were becoming a problem, and Mr Janakiev asked for Neli's help in mediating with Stefan's family as a last resort. Stefan's mother was working abroad, and he and his siblings were looked after by their father. The father worked as a lumberjack at night because he did not have a certificate to cut wood in the local forests. Stefan would often join his father at night and then he would miss school the next morning. Neli and I visited Stefan's home. 'I just don't like school. I can earn money like my father. I like to clean and feed our horse. I want to go to the forest,' he told us. Neli and I could not convince Stefan to go back to school. Stefan had decided that school was no longer necessary for him, since he wanted to follow in his father's footsteps and support the family economy. Stefan's father had become a labourer from an early age – so Stefan felt that to aspire to something different would be disloyal, almost as if he would disown his father if he tried to do 'better'. Just like Nikol, he had complete autonomy in making decisions about school. Stefan's case provides insights into the structural organisation of children's lives as regards education. Schools serve the reproduction of the 'dominant' culture, with the attitudes and behaviours of the subordinate group often excluded (Willis 1977).

Researching Roma children in different contexts presented their involvement in economic activities (Daskalaki 2004; Dunajeva 2017) and the provision of alternative forms of education inside the family (Okely 1997). Roma children are given moral autonomy to decide for themselves and to prioritise demands (Stewart 1997). Surely, such navigations needed good socio-emotional skills, which, in fact, schools are meant to teach. Instead, throughout the course of my research, I found that the biggest fear of the teachers was idleness or children being out of control or involved in criminal activities. 'Good' children needed to be influenced by people other than their parents – that is, those who were believed to carry a higher moral authority. Among kin, to be a 'good' child meant being a good daughter, sibling, son and grandchild and participating in the family economy. The importance of kinship was paramount, so children adjusted to navigate contradicting worlds and multiple demands.

Paradoxically, much attention is being focused on developing curricula to support Roma children through instruction and training, but there is less interest in what happens inside families and what children and parents perceive as moral and important. This disinterest leads to contradictions – a well-meant desire for inclusion results in exclusion and divisions in parallel worlds of different expectations. Indeed, the clash of different moralities and the contradictions they pose for the children is not necessarily known by both teachers and parents. These contradictions have various effects on children, and further research into this is needed. Nevertheless, it is my hope that by showing the many singular experiences, controversies, personal dilemmas, hopes and aspirations one can comprehend how complex, fragmented and yet unique Roma individuation is in response to state and kin values.

To Conclude

Going back to the main argument of this book, by providing a diversity of situations and characters, I wanted to illustrate how homogenising experiences, situations, persons and identities can lead to misunderstandings. The focal point of analysis in this chapter was to explore how and why the state acts in a particular way and how these actions affect the choices made by Roma parents and children regarding education. There was a universal assumption amongst the professionals in Radost that the critical role of schools is to teach morality, citizenship and discipline to all children. The disciplining force of these institutions (Bourdieu 1997; Fassin 2015) to organise time and space, roles and relations, was perhaps the most important resource of the state in its controlling and guiding role for a population. The granularity of invisible stories, the intimacy of kinship relationships, and the local expressions of culture often did not matter to the formal realm of the state. Whatever area we research, as Clark (2008) suggests, be it 'education or health, the states' activities regarding the care and control of its Gypsy and Traveller citizens often appear to be confused, shifting between the punitive and restrictive as well as being ill-informed and lacking any kind of joined-up coherent strategy' (ibid.: 66).It appears also that the contexts in which the state interventions and values operate are non-negotiable, but in fact both state and kin actors allow space for negotiation. Each of the stories presented here has something telling to offer. These stories belong to individuals who challenged the status quo – these are the few but committed teachers who saw children as equal, the parents who strove for what they believed can lead to a better future for their children inside or outside school and the children who bravely made difficult choices in regard to their education and families. I attempted to paint a highly fragmented picture, one that is familiar to the human condition, one that shows one's ability to live in the now and aspire to 'become' in the future.

Notes

1. Whilst I aim to contribute towards a less developed anthropological lacuna to give voice to Roma children, I also need to reflect on my positionality and access to research with children and the ethical dimension of it. My first and foremost ethical consideration was to make sure that I took all measures for the protection and safety of the children who were part of the research, both in institutional settings and in the Roma neighbourhoods. All conversations with children in the neighbourhood had an adult (a parent or guardian) present. It was essential that I had the children's informed consent to take part. The names of all children have been changed.
2. *Pomak* is a derogatory term and refers to a minority population residing in Bulgaria who converted to Islam during Ottoman rule.

CHAPTER 4

THE 'HYPERREAL' VIS-À-VIS THE 'EVERYDAY' ROMA
Identity and Activism

Growing up as a Roma child, I had some incredibly engaged role models to follow in my family. I remember my father painting the local Roma community centre during his annual leave and taking me with him to help. My mother encouraged me and my sisters to do well at school so we could 'help our people'. My grandmother told me: 'You may dream about other worlds, but you must never forget your beginnings.' She herself knitted socks and cardigans, which she gifted to the people in need in the Roma neighbourhood. My aunt, a preschool teacher, also encouraged me: 'If it is possible for me to dream, you can dream too'. Thus, I decided that I was going to become a nurse and help my people.

Upon my graduation from medical college, I applied for a job in the local hospital. Following this, the hospital director called me and informed me that although he was not disqualifying me from the application process, he needed the mayor's approval before offering me a job. The mayor had warned him to keep all jobs for people he approved of, including not giving any cleaning jobs to *tsiganite*. An application from a Roma nurse set a precedent in a small provincial town in the early 2000s. Apparently, the mayor used his control over state-funded jobs to make sure he had supporters for the next local election. My application was turned down, so I enrolled into further studies and commenced work at the regional nongovernmental organisation. This is when I was introduced to the civil society world of Roma activism. Naturally, years later when I commenced research, my first contacts in the field came from NGOs. Non-engagement was out of the question for me. I was expected and expected myself to be engaged, to give back to the community and to 'do good' (Fisher 1997). So, this chapter is as much about me as my informants. What I present here are themes that have been built into my existence for a long time. It was natural for me to be engaged in NGO work as I was driven to 'better', even change, the work of the state, and I illustrate here that this is indeed the grand intention of activism.

Again, in the same vein as in the previous chapters, I present a complex picture of fragmentation to challenge binary thinking and see value in the focus on the granular experience. The ethnographic material here shows instability, tensions and ambiguity but not only; these spaces, narratives and unstable categories can yield some highly productive discussion points (Lewis and Schuller 2017). I reflect on the 'emergence' of the Roma-related 'nongovernmental' (Van Baar 2018), and I interrogate the meaning of this 'supposedly unitary category'. Since activism is performed by a wide variety of actors in different professions: teachers, social workers, health mediators, researchers, economists – people of different hierarchical positions, of different ethnicity, gender and class – my goal is to show the diversity of narratives within the 'nongovernmental' category as a way of informing theory and practice. Importantly, just as the state is not monolithic (Abrams 2008) neither is the 'nongovernmental', and we ought to learn from this.

The NGO/humanitarian realm is often seen as a weak sector, 'but it is this weakness that is the source of its strength. It brings a moral sense to politics – although not without some ambiguity' (Fassin 2013: 37). NGO workers have multiple interests in the communities they work with – from purely altruistic and ideological to the perpetuation of Roma 'victimhood' (Guy 2013: 201) and ensuring continuity of NGO existence. I put forward the case for studying the ways in which humanitarianism (NGO-ism) shapes practices that support the development of policies and the power relations between those who help and the ones who are helped. I argue that Roma-related activism aims to correct the actions or non-actions of the state by re-creating its work vis-à-vis state processes, including emphasising bureaucratic practices as a reference (Lewis and Schuller 2017). NGO professionals may not be functioning as employees of the state, but they are instrumental in enacting government policies.

I also illustrate that engagement can have undesirable and contradictory effects and that it may also be the only alternative for Roma students and graduates, also called the 'Roma elite', to find professional realisation. Again, along the lines of the main idea of this book, I follow the plot of individuals in order to identify the many juxtaposed contexts through which identification in social life is empirically negotiated. Crucially, I value the importance of understanding the lifeworlds of both the NGO employees and the people they help. The stories in this chapter contain reflections on change in social status, expectations from within and outside the community, acceptance and identity choice. The individual stories, including my own, convey the multitude of complex social positions contained in the everyday. Undeniably, these narratives present contradictions and contestations.

The 'Nongovernmental Category'

NGOs are important political and civil actors of 'governmentality' (Ferguson and Gupta 2002; Foucault 1991), and states have come to view them as tools to increase power. The development of private civil society as service providers alongside the state was particularly important in the early postsocialist period. This is when NGOs were perceived as an alternative to the socialist welfare state being diminished in the most acute ways during the restructuring in the 1990s (Kaneff 2019). The withdrawal of the state had to be balanced, if only to a minuscule extent, by the offer of something else, and this was the NGO and 'know-how' sector (Lewis 2008; Van Baar 2018). NGOs became the vehicle for collective action and social change, and they were introduced as an integral part of neoliberalist policy.

Since 1989, there has been a massive development of NGOs that focus on Roma populations' access to education, employment, housing and health, among other things. This process is often called the 'ethnic awakening' and the rise of Roma 'ethnonationalism' (Gheorghe 1997). Different research sources point to Roma activism first being recorded in the 1970s, although there were forms of Roma activism prior to this (Marushiakova and Popov 2000). The World Roma Congress, the International Roma Union, and the Roma National Congress were established in the 1970s. Since the burgeoning of Roma civil society, the term Gypsy or *tsiganin* in Bulgaria and across other European countries has increasingly come to be seen as a pejorative term. It was not until communism fell that the term 'Roma' began to be used widely, including in policy language (Dunajeva 2014; Guy 2013). Civil society played an important role in contributing to the replacement of Gypsy or *tsigani* with Roma. This in itself is a remarkable achievement. Today in policy language and to a large degree in academia, on a wide geographical scale, communities are united under the umbrella term Roma, a term that has also come to be politically institutionalised by state and nonstate practices. Presenting Roma as one identifiable group with common attributes such as language, culture and common experience of discrimination is meant to create empowerment and social change.

Today, concepts such as 'Roma integration' and 'social inclusion' have become the common vocabulary of international nongovernmental and governmental organisations alike. Roma identity is conceptualised as 'ethnoclass' and focuses on the alleviation of poverty and improvement of the socioeconomic situation through education, housing and employment (Vermeersch 2012a, 2012b). While Roma were not part of the official and expert discourse prior to 1989, they have now become the main focus of political and scientific scrutiny (Surdu 2014). So, in a sense, Roma NGO activism is seen as empowering because of its engagement with identity politics and focus on policy influences for Roma inclusion.

Nevertheless, Roma activism has also been described as 'ethnobusiness', 'the Gypsy industry', 'NGO-isation' (Van Baar 2018: 37). Peter Vermeersch (2001: 16) ends one of his articles with the question 'How to build a movement on a spoiled identity?', referring to an identity that is stigmatised. Vermeersch contends that some Roma communities have become somewhat 'ambivalent' towards being associated with a 'spoiled' or 'project identity'. What the author means is that Roma in political terms have come to be associated with vulnerability, marginality, poverty, in 'need of saving' – an identity that is constructed not necessarily by the identity holders themselves. Well-educated Roma professionals, politicians, artists and others, 'who have become increasingly articulate' (Vermeersch 2001: 4), are responsible for the process of Roma mobilisation, including the creation of the 'Roma elite'. Although the number of activists has increased, authors suggest that they have disassociated from 'local knowledge' (Trehan 2001). Nonstate initiatives alike have promoted a specific image of Roma, a kind of representation that stems from political discourses that put 'the Roma' in a single and homogeneous group, without recognising internal differences and struggles, or class, ethnic, and gender differences. This promotion of one identity has been done in the hope of making 'the Roma problem' easier to solve (McGarry 2010). However, the heterogeneity of Roma communities causes tension between those who emphasise unity of interests and those who do not feel represented by an identity constructed on negative associations. NGOs may adapt to the discourses of government and other funding agencies while continuing to reinforce the construct of 'the Roma as a problem population' (Timmer 2010: 265).

In my work, I witnessed various aspects of the above interpretations and tendencies of NGO representation; however, I would like to think of the 'emergence' of this 'problematic identity' as a more complex phenomenon. Some of my informants considered themselves to be part of the 'Roma elite' and were intimately aware of the issues faced by their contemporaries, be they health, education, employment obstacles. Alienation and rejection of the grassroots, however, did happen, and I shall illustrate this through the life stories that follow. I argue that creating binaries and categories of engaged versus nonengaged, elite versus grassroots, 'for' or 'against' NGOs (Van Baar 2018: 28) may not be totally useful for theory, or more importantly, in practice, in having a positive effect on Roma lives. Through the very useful lens of ethnography, we can understand how everyday activism is performed, while interrogating the meanings behind it.

The 'Stupidity of Bureaucracy', the 'Hyperreal Roma' and 'the Gift'

'We know each other. We are a circle of people who have learned the stories of exclusion very well and keep repeating them from different angles' – said Stoyan, the leader of the NGO I volunteered for when I started fieldwork. Unfortunately, Stoyan could not express his frustrations with state and nonstate actors, as he was part of the system, one which 'feeds itself from the Roma problems', and being Roma himself he could not admit this to his community. Participants from Roma and pro-Roma NGOs, 'the usual suspects' as he called them, often gathered together to focus on the major areas for achieving 'Roma inclusion' – housing, health, education, etc. – and presented their experiences and arguments. Stoyan was frustrated:

> No change is happening. We speak but have no voice in a house of wolves who see Roma either as lambs or monsters. We use the same language, the same empty words everywhere. If only we had good anti-discrimination laws, inclusive curriculums in schools, empowered young people, jobs accessible to everyone ... It is all talk.

Stoyan's NGO was facing financial difficulties when I joined as a volunteer. Only three people were full-time staff members, including Stoyan himself, and two were working on a part-time basis. The NGO relied on volunteers as well as on the education and health mediators, who were paid by the local authorities. The local government was largely not funding his work, and Stoyan needed to raise funds from independent, mostly international grant-making organisations, various embassies in Bulgaria, state funding wherever available and European Union projects. This meant that the NGO was in competition with every other Roma-related Bulgarian and international NGO pursuing social development causes. It was difficult for Stoyan to juggle the management of the organisation because he took an active part in community outreach and the fundraising to sustain his staff members. Most of the project funding was on a short-term basis – from six months to two years. The stability of many NGOs in Bulgaria was similar, according to Stoyan, since there were very few self-sustaining organisations who could afford to 'speak for the people and not for someone else's interests'. To be independent was Stoyan's dream, and he worked tirelessly to find ways to sustain his organisation, including through local business ideas. Most of Stoyan's NGO funders were from Western Europe, and he doubted that the reliance on them would ever stop. After Bulgaria joined the European Union, some of the international NGOs based in the country left to support countries of a higher priority to development agencies. This is when Stoyan lost some of his most generous and flexible donors, who did not demand rigorous and long reporting.

I joined Stoyan's meetings with the Bulgarian branch of a well-known international children's rights organisation (INGO) that was funding one of Stoyan's educational projects. Stoyan needed to make regular reports to the INGO, who needed to be accountable as the lead applicant on a European Commission project – the larger donor – to ensure further funding. The INGO therefore requested three-monthly financial reports from Stoyan and weekly calls with him. Stoyan felt that although the INGO was the lead project applicant, the actual work with the community was ultimately left to him, so he asked for less emphasis on reporting in order to focus on the results of the project. However, the INGO saw his reaction as a sign of non-professionalism. Part of the reporting required information such as the number of Roma children and parents reached, stories of positive developments, photographs and videos.

Earlier in the project, Stoyan had sent detailed information and was now asking the INGO to space the reporting so he could focus on his project deliverables. The officer responsible for Stoyan's project required the approval of his manager, the director of the INGO. Unfortunately, the director was not available to speak to Stoyan, and we were assured that a decision would be communicated to Stoyan. He assumed that in the meantime the frequent reporting requirement had been dropped. This was not the case because later Stoyan understood that the INGO had decided to suspend project funding. Apparently, the officer had forgotten to ask the director for approval and funding was suspended based on the missed reporting. Stoyan apologised profusely and asked for renewal of funding. At the end of the day, it was his NGO that was not trusted and was seen as not sufficiently professional and needing more experience and capacity in order to comply with the 'bureaucratic' world of the INGO. Stoyan needed to create partnerships with well-established NGOs in Bulgaria and internationally, even though they did not necessarily know his community well, in order to be able to comply with funding requirements. No staff member of the INGO was Roma, however its core mission was to 'alleviate poverty and achieve social inclusion through the provision of education to minority children'. Stoyan also had to meet the INGO staff in their office, in the 'central' not the marginal territory of the Roma neighbourhood. Of course, the INGO needed to sustain itself, and NGOs like Stoyan's, working on the ground and providing 'real stories', were vital for their continuous existence. Stoyan, an economics graduate, on the other hand, found the INGO reporting requirements tedious, not relevant and simply 'stupid'.

Here I think of David Graeber's work on bureaucracy and its 'stupidity' in which he presents how bureaucratic principles are extended to every aspect of our existence, and how filling out forms has meant the bureaucratisation of everyday life (Graeber 2015: 27–32). Graeber analysed the procedures used by the state and talked about the police forces, 'who are empowered to impose arbitrary resolutions backed by the threat of force' (ibid.), but his analysis can be extended to nonstate institutions in order to illustrate how NGOs enact the idea of the state through documentation and in a way impose arbitrary 'symbolic violence' (Bourdieu 1991). Perhaps Graeber is right in summarising bureaucracy as 'a kind of war against the human imagination' (Graeber 2015: 82). The real issue in Stoyan's reporting conundrum was power; he was the 'unequal partner' in the project proposal. There was no understanding of the local context, and although the bureaucratic detail of reporting looked rational and ensured accountability and efficiency, it was arbitrary and indeed 'stupid'. 'Bureaucratic procedure invariably means ignoring all of the subtleties of real social existence and reducing everything to ... forms, rules, statistics, or questionnaires' (Graeber 2015: 75).

Little did the local Roma beneficiaries know that they were being presented as 'victims' (Gheorghe 2013), 'people on the margins', 'ignorant' subjects – people who needed parenting classes because they do not know how to look after their children, who in turn needed to be helped and educated, to be saved from poverty, discrimination and illiteracy. The very existence of poverty and discrimination is the survival path of the NGOs. According to Stoyan: 'We have created our own NGO industry and we depend on it. Since everyone is concerned about us Roma – international institutions, United Nations, European Union, governments, the West, you name it, we give them what they want.' Of course, Stoyan's insight is not unique. Anthropologists have explored this humanitarian phenomenon elsewhere. The self-preservation efforts of NGO actors in Brazil have led to the establishment of the 'hyperreal Indian', a social construction that ensures that the Indian population is perpetually presented as 'in need of saving', as vulnerable but also super real, something that transcends everyday life (Ramos 1994). 'But for most [NGOs], especially the well-established, defending Indians has become a sort of business enterprise, complete with market competition and publicity' (Ramos 1994: 162).

Often humanitarian aid representatives, health workers, nurses, doctors and social workers see themselves as 'gatekeepers' with regard to who legitimately deserves to be served by the nation-state and who does not and how moral it is to help or not help those in need (Tiktin 2011). Humanitarian aid recipients also must 'perform' to be able to fit into state, cultural and social expectations. This performance creates more inequalities, complications and grey areas, with the solution ultimately boiling down to the support of bureaucratic procedures. Where inequalities reach high levels, human-itarianism (NGO-ism) provides a certain moral stance, some solidarity of sort and glimpses of consciousness (Fassin 2013: 37). Children living in pov-erty, especially those who are not accessing state education, such as Roma children, perfectly fit with bureaucratic notions of 'vulnerability' and what is deemed as requiring humanitarian action. Exactly because of this moral stance, humanitarianism or 'the nongovernmental' has become 'untouch-able', with the moral intentions of NGO workers justifiable. For many NGOs, 'the hyperreal' Roma are 'an appropriate working hypothesis', the ultimate 'ethical hologram' (Ramos 1994: 163).

Ultimately, NGOs depend on external funding, and they are more accountable to their funders than the people they work with and for. As Stoyan himself suggests, Roma NGO representatives are themselves not above the process of convincing funding institutions to support the solu-tion to Roma 'problems'. Despite meaning well, they also find themselves in a precarious situation, being forced to 'co-opt' (Mirga-Kruszelnicka 2015; Trehan 2001) – that is, cooperate in creating 'the hyperreal' Roma in order to ensure financial sustainability. Here I must clarify that I am not referring to the many grassroots Roma-led initiatives, such as the mother's initiative in Sastipe and active volunteer groups, which so far have evaded the bureau-cratic complex network of NGOs and international agencies. The everyday Roma exist and are in close contact with these social structures.

One may ask what the role of the donors is. Having worked for the largest private philanthropy investing in 'Roma inclusion', I feel that I need to add the donor perspective here too. Donors have interests, be it to satisfy account-ability criteria, or to satisfy compassion, solidarity, emotions, organisational strategies, state plans, etc. Being interested in community development, social justice and human rights – organisationally, personally and emotionally – donors use grant-making and project funding strategically. Marcel Mauss's analysis, although it applies to 'functions of exchange in archaic societies', is highly useful in helping us understand the relationship between giver and receiver. Gifting is always relational and carries consequences. European Union funding may broadly aim to achieve the social cohesion, equality and well-being of European citizens, but it also comes with specific rules and regulations for funding applications. These can often require a higher degree of accountability mechanisms, including strong financial and administra-tive capacities. Various philanthropies may justify their moral, humanitarian emotions and beliefs through elaborate strategies, requiring flexibility and efficient social change to prove possibilities to national governments. Gov-ernment funds may have specific criteria for size, administrative capacity and influence of the NGOs they fund. Often what these have in common is that they look for the 'elites', those who can eloquently speak 'local knowledge' (Geertz 1985). In return, those who are given grants must reciprocate 'gifts' – that is, stories of misfortune, victimhood and images and documentation of poverty, but also success stories and situations of social change. The function of documentation, reporting, monitoring and evaluation thus is not only about accountability, auditing and following administrative procedures; it is also about securing further gifts or grants in the future. Much can be traced in documents, such as project funding proposals for 'Roma inclusion', reports, photos and so on. These can be sites that provide more information on the aspect of 'gifting', humanitarianism and bureaucracy.

Activism, Authenticity and Identity

I began this chapter with my personal story and what led me to Roma activism. The reasons were complex. On the one hand, there were the expectations of my family and community. On the other hand, my own aspirations, the desire to 'do good', to see change in the lives of my contemporaries, the expectations of my teachers and the lack of local employment opportunities all created the social conditions for me to be involved in activism. I chose to identify as Roma, and I was identified as such. Reflexively, perhaps I also strived to be authentic by responding to my own expectations and those of my community, family and friends. The question 'Are you really Roma?' externally, and the motivation within my community and kin to 'show that Roma can study and do well also' conditioned me to think of my activism as being genuine, as exemplifying authenticity and proving that my achievements and my Roma-ness were genuine. Authenticity, however, I find impossible to theorise as it can have a multiplicity of meanings and interpretations (Acton 1998; Lindholm 2008; Theodosiou 2008).

Activism is occupied with the authenticity and the survival of the group, the community; in this case, the shared Roma identity, to counter negative preconceptions. Hence the tendency is to focus on the individual as part of 'the group' rather than on the individual as an exemplar. In this section, I follow the individual, somewhat highly personal stories of my informants in order to identify the many times through which identification in social life is negotiated. I believe that just as I am motivated by 'altruistic values', by care, consideration and compassion for others so are my activists informants, but they also strive to prove their authenticity inside kin and community and externally with friends, peers, colleagues, funders, state and nonstate. Because it is only when we are recognised by others, and when we acquire a positive understanding of ourselves, that we are able to express freely who we are or, to put it in other words, to realise ourselves, to achieve personhood by countering discrimination, repression and extreme intervention through the mode of activism. So, being engaged in Roma activism can come as a predisposition, in a way as a middle ground whereby a person can satisfy and comply with the requirements of community belonging, of the personal conviction to counter discrimination, whilst having an opportunity to work in a well-known 'insider' terrain and realise self-potential. Of course, this can be contested, but not listening to the personal narratives of activists and not considering their motivations renders discussions of activism one-sided and limiting.

Here I present the internal struggles for employment and how being educated can present contradictions. The stories of the students, graduates and professionals, often seen as the elites, show a diversity of social situations and temporalities that we can learn from. I also show that being a Roma university student or graduate represents an opportunity as well as a challenge. These Roma navigate the separate and often isolated spheres of home – within kinship relationships and community life – and outside in the state domain of school, university and work. While Roma students may be expected to sustain and reproduce their Roma-ness inside the community (where there may be fears of assimilation and cultural loss), externally they can be rejected or find that they need to negotiate access by identifying differently, including by rejecting their Roma identification. In order to achieve their aspirations without encountering discrimination, Roma can choose to hide their origin – from classmates, peers, colleagues and teachers – by 'acting Bulgarian' or completely ceasing connections with anything to do with 'being Roma'. Becoming an activist does not necessarily guarantee cultural alienation from the community, and being an activist does not always guarantee upward social mobility either. These professionals can also choose to leave activism, work for the state, go abroad, return to activism and so on. The choice is important here; it is agency that we need to consider when discussing Roma activism (Beck and Ivasiuc 2018).

Stoyan's Ideology

> People don't realise how hard I had to work to get to where I am. My motivation is to help.

Stoyan had obtained an Economics degree and was the first university graduate in his family with a diploma from the prestigious 'Karl Marx' Higher Institute of Economics in Sofia. The fall of communism meant that after he graduated he was free to own a business, and he set up a profitable pastry-making venture. However, in a short period of time, Stoyan's business had grown so significantly that his competition in the region began to lobby the local authorities to intervene. His factory was inspected more often than usual, the administrative burdens increased and he began to receive personal threats from people who he believed were his business competition. One morning on the way to work, he saw a note on the broken window of his car saying '*Tsiganino* (Gypsy), give up. Think of your family! We will break you.' Stoyan had two daughters and a wife he needed to protect. Not long after this threat, the local authority health and safety inspectors put impossibly high sanctions on his pastry-making business, and he was forced to go into administration. This is when Stoyan vowed to become an activist for Roma rights. He set up an organisation that focused on access to education. He was able to obtain initial funding from various embassies in Bulgaria and managed to visit other countries on experience exchange.

In the first years of postsocialism, Stoyan's NGO focused on improving literacy in one of Bulgaria's largest Roma neighbourhoods. Schools began to be seen not as the only provider of education as in socialist times, as nonstate actors provided alternative forms of education to support Roma children to achieve better at school (Dunajeva 2017). These changes led to states no longer being the exclusive educator. The collapse of communism affected many Roma children, and in Stoyan's words:

> The system simply wasn't working anymore. No schools looked for the absent children, and the parents were more concerned with what their children were going to eat than sending them to school. Many went hungry for days. I had to help, I had to become an activist. It will be nearly 25 years since I began this work. I wake up thinking of the struggles of my people and go to bed with their problems. At times this is too much for my family. But for me, what I do gives me the chance to work and do what I love ... to help.

Stoyan gradually involved his wife in helping him, and they managed to reach a high number of Roma children who were not attending school. Stoyan's work expanded into the region, and his NGO team became a first point of contact for both the local authorities and the community. He sometimes endured criticism from his community because he was seen to be 'too close to the Bulgarians', but activism for him was imagined as work intended to bring about social and political change, no matter how he was perceived. It was his experience that counted, and he was willing to sacrifice time and risk rejection internally and externally. His involvement in activism was also personal. Indeed, activism was the result of the nexus between his personal life experiences and the ideologies he believed in, those of defending human rights, or simply 'doing good'.

Neli's Commitment

I was rebelling against anything and everything that people had made to be Roma.

Neli worked for Stoyan's NGO and, according to Stoyan, was his 'most committed employee'. She worked tirelessly to see the children in her Roma neighbourhood achieve at school. Wherever Neli went, children would follow her. Children knocked on her door at all times of day, including late in the evening, to ask for help with homework, to show her their student books, to ask her for food or simply to greet her. I knew this because I shared accommodation with Neli at her parents' house in Radost. Neli was not always this way, however. It was hard for me to believe that there was a time when she wanted to distance herself from Roma and her Roma identity. At school, she chose not to play with Roma children, and since she had a mother who was light-skinned, children rarely questioned her half-Bulgarian origin, although both parents in fact identified as Roma.

She enrolled into a traditional Bulgarian folklore group to ensure that her 'Bulgarian-ness' (*bulgarshtina*) was well accepted and studied the Bulgarian language and literature at university. 'Being Bulgarian' had to manifest in every area of her life, including how she looked. She cut her hair short because long hair was 'typical of the *tsiganski* women', she wore expensive, not too colourful clothes because *tsiganite* liked 'loud colours'; and wearing gold jewellery was a '*big no*' because this is how '*tsiganite* showed off'. She lost weight because Roma girls 'were plump', and she found a job in an accountancy company where no one knew that she was Roma and began saving money towards buying an apartment outside the Roma neighbourhood. Later, she had a Bulgarian boyfriend to whom she got engaged, but a discussion one day made her rethink her relationship with him and what she felt about her Roma identity.

I thought that I had nothing to do with the people who I grew up with, including my own family. I despised everything Roma. Things started to change when my Bulgarian fiancé told me that he didn't want my relatives to come to our wedding. He thought that since I hardly associated with them, there was no point in inviting them. I didn't react immediately but in the next couple of months something changed in my thinking. I was hurt. It's silly that I hadn't thought about this before, but suddenly I began considering how I would tell my children that their grandparents live in a Roma quarter and also how would my husband treat me in the future if he didn't think much of my parents now. We separated not long after, but this experience taught me that I needed to embrace who I was, my family, my community and the people who really cared for me.

Neli 'passed' as a Bulgarian for a long time. Her parents were concerned that in 'acting Bulgarian' (*pravi se na bulgarka*) she had grown apart from them and was navigating a different world isolated from their own. They never knew that she was engaged, although they had their suspicions she was in a relationship when Neli presented a male friend to them as a colleague. Once her relationship broke down, Neli began to spend more time in the Roma neighbourhood. She had graduated from university with a degree in Bulgarian linguistics and commenced helping the neighbourhood children with their homework. Stoyan was looking for volunteers in his NGO, and this is how she found herself 'involved in what people now call activism, but it is commitment'. Gradually, she involved her non-Roma business and education contacts in contributing to the work of the NGO, including by organising fundraising events, ensuring access to the local non-Roma *chitalishte* for performances by Roma children and liaising with the local banks for business loans to Roma entrepreneurs. For Neli, activism was a way of life that she had consciously chosen in relation to her past of denying her Roma-ness.

Sasha's Passion

> It is not easy for young Roma people today. University is more achievable, but jobs are not.

Sasha graduated as the *otlichnik* (excellent student) of her Public Relations university course. It had been two years since she graduated, and after a number of job applications she found a six-month internship opportunity through the support of Stoyan's NGO. The internship was based in the communications department of the city council. Although initially she was promised a permanent contract once her internship finished, she was not hired. She later learned from the cleaner of the building, whom she befriended because of her early starts and late finishes, that the mayor's secretary 'could not bear the thought of having a *tsiganka* in the most representative office in the city'. Sasha was later elected as the youngest (age 22) municipality councillor by the locals. Her participation in local government was seen as a positive and encouraging step by the Radost community, but she felt that 'being a role model' was a huge burden of representation, in that she always needed to consider the interests of the community before her own. Internally in her family and community, Sasha felt that the pressure was too much.

> If you fail, you disappoint your community. You need to be a role model for the children, for the youth, everyone basically. People think that when one finishes university, they can find a job and do better. I got education and I was doing all these community tasks, but I didn't have any money in my pocket. I was relying on my parents to help me.

For Sasha, to be educated against the odds but not be able to secure employment following her studies was not only a personal failure but as if she had failed all Roma. Sasha did not have a scholarship and relied on her parents to help her financially. She had also taken a loan, and this put her in a worse financial situation than before she began studying. There is an expectation that higher education will accommodate social mobility and employment access for Roma students, but in reality, this does not happen necessarily (Durst et al. 2014; Durst and Nyíro 2018). When I first met Sasha, she was considering leaving Bulgaria for an agricultural job in the Netherlands. She saw that the lack of employment opportunities and realisation after graduation was the main motivation to continue her activism. Sasha eventually got hired on a part-time basis in Stoyan's NGO, which was also her professional realisation, but more than that it was Sasha's way to counter discrimination. She was hopeful for the future.

Ekaterina's Choice

Ekaterina was one of the four children of Sherifa, a woman who was known to have come from a different part of Bulgaria and who the locals referred to as a 'different type of *tsiganka*'. Sherifa was seen as a tough woman, which I naively thought was because she rarely smiled. Sherifa told me that Ekaterina was a studious child. She excelled at school and expressed a wish to become a doctor. Her high school teacher, the wife of the Radost communist mayor, helped her to prepare for the exams and arranged for a university reference from her husband. Ekaterina also needed to be involved in the local *chitalishte* in order to receive a reference from the mayor and to secure a scholarship to go to medical school. In the 1960s, the Communist Party had introduced a policy to encourage more minority students in Bulgaria to study medicine. At the weekends and during her summer vacations, Ekaterina supported the leader of the Roma *chitalishte*. She helped with the preparations for the Bulgarian folklore concerts in the neighbourhood, most of which coincided with Roma traditional celebrations on these days and were attended by the local communist dignitaries. She was seen by both Roma and non-Roma as a young representative of the community. She was also chosen to be the Komsomol[1] secretary of her class, and in her mother's words she became 'the pride of our people'. In due course, Ekaterina was accepted to study medicine in Sofia. State education was free of charge, but Ekaterina's parents could not afford to visit her or help her financially with any additional costs. Her father was a shepherd, and he hardly came back home, while her mother was a cleaner in the local grocery store. She told me the following:

I never believed that Katia [Ekaterina] was going to be a doctor. I thought the whole thing was a joke and that the teachers were simply lying to her that she can study. They said good things about her at school but neither I nor her father went to school, so we couldn't understand and help her in any way. We couldn't give her money or help her with anything. I couldn't read ... All of a sudden then she just forgot about us. She took us, her sisters, her father and me, out of her heart and stamped on us as if we never existed ... Her father sold some sheep, and I went to Sofia. I asked and asked many people how to find her school but finally I was there. I asked the cleaner of the school how to find Katia, and she asked me to wait. I waited on the stairs while the passing by students looked at me as if I had fallen from the sky. At last she came out of the classroom; she took my hand, and we went out of the building. Then she embraced me, and she said that I should never visit her again. You see, she was well dressed, beautiful, and white and clean like a Bulgarian, and I was wearing my rugs of clothes, dirty *tsiganka* who couldn't say two words properly.

Ekaterina pursued her studies and became a doctor; however she vowed to never come back to Radost or contact her parents, sisters and relatives. Sherifa never saw her daughter again. This is why the locals thought of Sherifa as a 'tough' woman – she had lost not only a child but endured the embarrassment of her daughter's 'forgetting about who she was'. Ekaterina's sister once traced her to a hospital in Sofia, but Ekaterina refused to meet with her. Her family understood that Ekaterina had married another doctor, and no one knew anything more about her.

I heard the story of Ekaterina a number of times from different people in the Radost neighbourhood, largely because her story was given as a terrible example. It had left a lasting impression not only on her family but on her friends and community. It was obvious that this was a success story in one way, yet an utterly tragic example in another. This communal memory, this 'wound', as her friend Elza called it, was not to be forgotten. Amongst the Roma of Radost, Ekaterina became the antithesis, the opposite of what one was supposed to do and to become. Becoming someone else and forgetting one's roots were equal to a crime, even murder. Although, Ekaterina's story may seem at odds with the life stories presented earlier, her activism (despite complying with the spread of communist ideologies) was one of the reasons for her social mobility. Ekaterina's example also affected the locals' predisposition to activism and education. Parents whose children were doing well at school, including Neli's and Sasha's, would make sure to tell them about Ekaterina's story. Indeed, when Neli decided to downplay and 'erase her Roma-ness' she remembered Ekaterina's example.

This story of de-kinning highlights a number of elements and contradictions – the support of the local authorities and Ekaterina's teacher, her obligation and the pressure on her to represent her community and the way the community perceived her. For the neighbourhood and among kin, Ekaterina had achieved nothing but the worst possible thing – 'culture closure' (Gay y Blasco 2011). Yet, in another way she was a pioneer. She was the first Roma woman in Radost to go to university, the first Roma doctor from Radost, a person who managed to defy poverty, a professional who rose to the highest ranks of communist life and beyond. Ekaterina's story is an example of a professional Roma who chose to pass as non-Roma, perhaps out of fear of being discriminated against and being seen as different or simply to defy her family. Perhaps identification was a contradiction to her, or perhaps to her identification meant that 'being Roma' was 'no halfway position' but all or nothing (Williams 2003). Ekaterina's case remained a puzzle to me, but I am certain there are more stories like hers. Ekaterina's story provoked me not because it is unusual for a Roma to become a doctor but because she managed to achieve a complete breakaway with incredible force and a rupture of relationships. Somewhere in her life story was her activism. I wanted to visit Ekaterina in Sofia to share that she was not alone, that there were other Roma who had managed to navigate the world within and outside of the Radost neighbourhood, that these other people were doing their best to consolidate their pasts and futures. Sadly, I later learned that she had died of cancer alone, with no family around her.

There are many ideas that can be inferred from Stoyan's, Neli's, Sasha's and Ekaterina's narratives. Being educated is strongly linked to activism. Being 'educated' is a loose term here, and it encompasses not only university students and graduates but the concept of being literate and possessing skills seen by the dominant culture as enablers of societal inclusion. It is these skills that mean people are expected to give back to the community as the Roma 'elite' (Mirga and Georghe 1997; Vermeersch 2001, 2006). In fact, there is the expectation in both activism and academia that the Roma elite should give back to their communities without contesting their representation of the community (McGarry 2010: 10), but there are those who cannot bear the 'burden of representation', including its hyper-reality, inscribed on them either internally among kin and community or externally. Certainly, there are everyday Roma who have enforced self-representation (McGarry 2014: 8), but there are also those of us, as researchers and activists, who have not considered this agency that Roma can have in choosing to become what they aspire to.

To Conclude

This chapter can be seen as providing only a partial exploration of Roma activism. However, as in other chapters, I find that I am drawn towards the density of experience, the complex webs of meaning-making, the richness of open-endedness in the local. In presenting the above narratives, I attempted to challenge assumptions of Roma NGO moralities as purely selfish. I also urged that taking the side of the 'good local Roma' over the 'bad Roma elite' or 'the vulnerable Roma' over the 'bad non-Roma outsider' is not productive either. Through the ingenuity of ethnographic tools here, I showed that we need to engage in understanding the motives of Roma activism better and that identification with people whose situations are different from our own is not 'as transparent or unproblematic as we think' (Hall 1997). Activism draws heavily on identification. My informants made choices, crossed boundaries and achieved dreams and goals; some were discriminated against, and others negotiated acceptance or severance of relationships inside and outside kinship and community. Some decided to pursue opportunities elsewhere, outside of the NGO world, and others saw this as their motivation to contribute to 'do good'. Ultimately, what I surmise is that when we discuss Roma activism, we need to leave room for self-determination and self-realisation. Offering insights into the experiences of the individual, looking at the detail, the contradictions, can be illuminating.

Note

1. The Komsomol was a political structure entirely involved with the organisation and indoctrination of youth. The Komsomol or the Communist League of Youth was established for young people aged 14 to 28 who would eventually become future members of the Communist Party.

CHAPTER 5

HOME AND THE 'KINNING' STATE

When I think about home, there is one childhood memory that appears in my mind. 'Mum, I can't go any further. I am tired' – I said. 'Only a few more steps, you can do it' – my mother said, breathing heavily while carrying my younger sister on her back. We were climbing some broken concrete steps on a steep hill leading towards a place called 'the home'. It looked like this place was in a small forest, or at least this is how it seemed to me at age ten. From afar, I remember seeing walls covered in patches of peeling dark blue, white and grey paint and large graffiti letters next to signs that I was not supposed to see. The old building was empty, its doors and windows were broken. A man in a digger was working on the site, and he shouted at us to stay away. We sat on a broken wooden bench outside for what seemed to be an exceptionally long time. My mother stared at 'the home' while tears were rolling down her cheeks. Her 'home' was being demolished. Suddenly, this decrepit-looking building, once called 'home' not only by my mother but by thousands of other children, had become part of my own sense of home and family history.

I often think of what home means. Home is not just about the country in which one is born, nor is it only about the buildings, the spaces, the rooms, the furnishings and the materiality of space. Home is also about the people, the memories and the secrets that inhabit and make those material spaces feel like home. Home does not have a single meaning – it is 'a unique eternal truth of a place' (Massey 1994: 119). Home can refer to beginnings, memories and the past and as such is in flux. As well as a place or a point in time, home can be an existential position and an emotional arrival. Home can be about 'cultural norms and individual fantasies' (Rapport and Dawson 1998: 8). Home can also be connected to the notion of what it means to be away from home (Hannerz 2002). Home can be a space of intimacy, joy, family, social relationships and 'the stillness of place' (Howarth 2019; Pine 2007). Home can be a place of sadness, raw emotions, loneliness, abuse, arguments, secrets, all things pertaining to the private domain, to the household, that which composes kin relationships, intimacy and autonomy. But what happens when 'home' is literary and symbolically built and taken over by the state? Does the state become private, or does kinship become public? What if one must live their life in the public domain, with no recourse to all the privileges, responsibilities, highs and lows of kin relations and, instead, the state becomes their kin? Is home, the private and the 'counterpublic' a myth (Warner 2002)? 'How do people transform givenness into choice so that the world into which they are thrown becomes a world that they can call their own' (Jackson 1995: 123)?

Here I reflect on the dramatic over-representation of Roma children who lived and continue to live in care institutions in Bulgaria. The ethnographic material is based on observations and interviews with children in care homes, parents, state professionals and care leavers.[1] I reached some of them through the organisation I worked for, and others I reached through friends, family and local community initiatives. I return to the inter-relationship of kinship and state as I illustrate how policies targeted to help the children seen as most vulnerable in a population can marginalise those children even further. The chapter is structured as a journey of historical phases that have characterised Bulgaria to date – socialism, postsocialism and neoliberalisation.[2] Methodologically, I continue to argue that people can obtain 'a sense of agency, voice, and belonging' through composing their own stories as an empowering act (Jackson 2002: 185). In historical terms, I am also reminded that 'people's lives, even in the most barren of settings and contexts, involve hope as well as despair, agency and choice as well as coercion' (Pine 2018: 4). I follow unexpected stories told by children, who are rarely reflected in research.

The Concrete Care of the State

The 'home' in which my mother grew up – a large, monolithic concrete building with tall windows and wide doors – was purposed for hundreds of children who came from different parts of Bulgaria. Building such homes, indeed the building of all homes, identical blocks of apartments, vast housing estates, virtually the same-looking buildings for the proletariat, was part of the grandiose industrialisation and urbanisation projects of socialist Bulgaria (and elsewhere in the Soviet Union). The aim was to build a socialist nation, and this was thought through in detail, including the details of physical architectural styles (Kaneff 1995, 2019). At the beginning of socialism, building was dictated by a specific architecture style called Socialist Realism or Stalinist architecture, which was a combination of art and design forms 'to educate and inspire the proletariat' (Kelleher 2009: 62). Such examples of buildings are still accommodating government officials in Sofia today. Later, after Stalinism was denounced in the Soviet Union, Socialist Realism architecture was seen as excessive and exchanged in favour of Socialist Modernism, whereby communist states increased cheap construction at a quick rate. The Bulgarian landscape, as in other Eastern European countries, was transformed. The green agricultural land shaft of the cities was now dominated by the high-rise buildings of concrete apartment blocks (*panelki*). Concrete was going to house the proletariat and strengthen socialism, and the strengthening of socialism required the moving of the masses from the villages of rural Bulgaria to the cities to begin mass production rather than serve self-economy (Stoykova 2006).

The totalitarian state was not only building people's material homes, but it was also working on influencing what was happening inside their homes, within the kin domain (Pine 2002, 2003). The construction of a socialist society, including its literal concrete mass building, involved the creation of an extended family and social kinship through institutions and ideology (Khlinovskaya Rockhill 2010). Dealing with women's economic independence and liberation from the grip of the bourgeoisie ideology became a priority. The argument that women had to become equal to men – that is, be free to participate in the labour market – helped the promotion of the so-called 'socially responsible parenthood' (Engels 1972). Indeed, by the 1960s, pressing demands for improved living and working conditions propelled the issue of work-care integration onto the political agendas of all Eastern European socialist states (Rajkai 2014). The family came to be viewed as being incapable of providing proper childcare and raising children as approved socialist citizens. Childcare needed to be shared between the family and numerous public institutions whereby children would be looked after by professionally trained, non-related adults (Khlinovskaya Rockhill 2010). Indeed, as once famously put by the pedagogue Makarenko, these state agents were the 'engineers of human souls' in working alongside the parents and through the parents (Bowen 1962).

The ideology of the time asserted that the inequality of the family partners (a man and a woman) would be destroyed, and the family as an institution would no longer be a contract in capitalist terms; rather, it would operate in the spirit of comradeship between two equal persons (Stoykova 2006: 2). In practice, this reinforced the differences of families and persons who did not fit within the socialist family ideology. Single parents, those living in poverty and those with children born out of wedlock, amongst others, were deemed 'inadequate'. Their children needed to be 'homed' elsewhere. Roma parents and their children also found themselves in that category of 'unfit', imperfect families, being vulnerable and not strong enough to cement the moral future of the nation. There was no place for imperfection and weakness; the strength of this moral and physical concrete, the strength of socialism was paramount.

The memories, traces and experiences embedded in the buildings of socialist Bulgaria were shared by my informants. A large grey concrete building must have looked rather terrifying to a young child. Kiril (age 53) was five years old when he was taken to a children's home approximately 70 km away from the place where his single mother lived. His first memory of the institution was the large building.

> I would often lose myself in the corridors until older children found me and took me back to my classroom ... I hated the winters there. They were very cold because the building was a huge block of concrete. We slept in one large bedroom with more than fifty beds and with only one small stove to warm us. The younger children had to put firewood in the stove and the older children were taking their blankets, leaving the little ones without covers.

One may argue that just as the massive concrete and metal statues and monuments raised across the country were there to remind people of the socialist progress and the powerful Soviet Bloc, so were the children's homes. They were there to remind families that inadequate child upbringing had its consequences and that the state could do kinship better and bigger. These communal buildings were essentially positioning a community of young strangers with no common ties or kin into one space, one home, one private and intimate realm. How insulated or accessible the building was did not matter as much as what this 'home' was going to produce – community, comradeship and moral citizenship. In reality, what Kiril experienced was somewhat different:

> I remember the beatings and harassment of the older children towards the younger children. The younger children had to make the beds of the older children, wash their underwear and socks by hand, and there was no hot water. Those slippery concrete floors in the bathroom in the winter were so dangerous.

Still, Kiril believed that the state gave him more opportunities than his mother would have been able to provide if he had stayed with her in the Roma neighbourhood. Safka, Kiril's mother, went to school in the 1940s but never finished elementary education. She married early and by the age of twenty-one had three children in addition to looking after an ill husband. When Kiril was three months old, Safka's husband died, and she was forced to return home to her maternal family.

> I was left without a choice. I was a widow with three young children, and the state offered to look after them. After the death of my husband, I had to go back to my

family, but I could not stay there for long. My brother had his own family, and my children and I shared a room with my mother. I began working in the local agriculture cooperative, but the money was so little. My only choice was to send my children to the home and start saving to build my own home. The director of the home assured me that they would be well cared for.

Care often carries a moralising connotation that is related to people's social lives, to the political and legal regulation of life and to society in general (Howell 2006; Thelen and Haukanes 2010). The economic and symbolic value of the state's decision to look after children had to serve a purpose – to provide safety, refuge, food and education. These homes, also called orphanages, largely accommodated social orphans (i.e. children who had at least one living parent and all children without parental care)[3] and were created to provide safety for children, and this process was not unique to Bulgaria.[4]

In response to high infant mortality and poverty at the beginning of socialism (1944) and after the Second World War, following in the footsteps of the Russian Bolshevik government, the newly formed Bulgarian socialist government also sought to feed and raise the nation's children (Ball 1993; Mihaylov 2020). Although the state envisioned itself as a welfare state concerned with the care of its subjects, it was in the formation of socialist childhoods – in other words, the upbringing of loyal socialist workers of the future – where the state's other aim lay. The rapid building and development of children's homes (*detski domove*) was also dictated by a political ideology that encouraged the disintegration of patriarchy and the withdrawal from the household economy (Pine 2002). These institutions were seen as far better equipped than the 'bourgeois' family to fashion children into productive, devoted members of communist society (Khlinovskaya Rockhill 2010). Single Roma mothers like Safka, who lacked education, far from fitting the bourgeoisie image, were seen as highly 'unprepared' to produce socialist moral citizens. Although Safka's children were reunited with her when Kiril was ten years old, it was not unusual for children to remain in care until they reach the age of eighteen. Long-term placements, dictated by the supposition that the child was not going to be returned to the family, were the norm.

The creation of homes for different age groups – baby homes (age 0–3), young children's homes (age 3–7), homes for children and adolescents (age 7–18) – ensured a transition into adulthood through the care home system (Mihaylov 2020). Other homes such as those for children with disabilities were also established. Safka recalled that there was no child in her Roma neighbourhood not going to some form of *pansion*, a term that encompassed special schools for children with disabilities or orphanages where food and accommodation were provided. But how did the state encourage parents to give up their children so straightforwardly? The state drew on the powerfully evocative language of kinship (Pine 2018) – such as 'home' (*dom*) and 'the mother state' (*darzhavata majka*) – to prove its moral character and its long-term kinning ability. Adoption was possible, but it was reserved mostly for what was known to be healthy and 'light-skinned' children from the baby homes according to Julian (age 45), who told me: 'Children with disabilities were not wanted for adoption. I think I was not adopted because I was born to a *tsigansko* [Gypsy] family, so I was darker, and I also suffered from problems with my feet.'

Managing disability was done by confinement and placement in baby homes and then homes for children and adults with disabilities. Disability was seen as the inability to work and engage in wage labour, so the state took over the care of people deemed unproductive (Mladenov 2015). There was no place for self-production, self-realisation, private interests and household economy; simply put, everything that was capitalist in nature, and bourgeois individualism had to be diminished and uprooted. The 18-year-old care leavers who finished school and were deemed productive – in other words, those without disabilities – were allowed to venture into the communal socialist world of work. Consider the case of Violeta, who was in care in the late 1960s and who is now a teacher:

> When I finished high school my class teacher asked me to go to her office. She was clearly worried about something. She sat me down and said that I was an excellent student and that she didn't want to document me as a *tsiganka* on my student record. 'I will write that you are of Bulgarian origin so that this doesn't prevent you from going to university. You didn't grow up amongst the *tsigani* anyway. You grew up in a home, and it is fair that I don't write this down. I need you to promise me that what I do will not be discussed further'.

The socialist upbringing was a purposeful intellectual, cultural and moral development, and it involved the moulding of children's worldviews into socialist values (Khlinovskaya Rockhill 2010). But it also de-reified identification. Anyone who identified differently in terms of ethnicity, gender, ability and so on was risking their successful integration into a socialist society. Violeta was given a 'blank card' to venture into the world as something other than being Roma, as an adequate, moral socialist citizen – qualities not seen as *tsiganski*. The formation of an individual was envisioned to become completely inseparable from societal goals, with the state existing not only outside but also inside each individual (Verdery 1996). If Violeta had identified as Roma, she would have risked estrangement from the values of socialism, which ideologically postulated that there were no differences between people. At the forefront of the ideologically minded socialists was not only to support individuals like Violeta, who was the progeny of *tsigani* parents, but also to supplant their identification with that of the socialist ideal. In practice, Violeta's identification as Roma came down to her genetic make-up; she was called '*the tsiganka* teacher' because of her darker skin and because she had returned to her home in the Roma neighbourhood. Socialism was not void of racism, and since even Marx was perplexed by the subject of race in his 'Eastern Question' and wrote that the Balkans were populated by a 'conglomerate of different races and nationalities, of which it is hard to say which is the least fit for progress and civilization' (Marx and Aveling 1891: 4), what could be expected of the ordinary followers of socialism in Bulgaria?

Still, Violeta was appreciative of what 'the home' had given her. She had taken part in an array of well-organised, state-run extra-curricular activities, such as free summer camps, excursions and afterschool classes. She had also participated in compulsory agricultural harvest brigades, involving heavy physical labour. The main goal had been to raise a person in whom 'the norms of communist morals turned into personal beliefs and formed the basis of everyday behaviour' (Mihaylov 2020). Violeta told me: 'We had rotas, everything was done in order. We washed dishes in the kitchen and cleaned the canteen premises and the yard. We collected firewood and maintained the fire in the stoves and many other tasks. We were busy in the day, doing all sorts of activities ...' Perfection, strength and moral character had to be lived through 'self-government' (*samoupravlenie*), which meant that children took on daily chores to acquire a sense of control over their lives and an instinct for collectivism and comradeship (Ball 1993).

The capacity for self-governance was a concept widely applied to the education of Roma children during socialism but also later in postsocialism. While everyone and anything was audited because the spheres of home, private, communal and public converged inside the 'homes', children like Violeta witnessed the imperfect side of the moral socialist state. Paradoxically, the state 'audit culture' (Strathern 2000) was relevant for monitoring the family and kin setting, but it was not fit for auditing the experiences of children themselves inside the state homes. Violeta shared the following:

> There were so many nights which we spend in silent sobs under the cold covers. The fear of the dark after the designated curfew; the shouting of the educator in the morning, the slamming of the wooden bedroom door, and the stressed, half-awake children, rushing and bumping into each other to go wash. There were only five sinks with ice-cold water for all the hundred and twenty children who lived on the ground floor. Imagine the same picture on all five floors of the building. It was as if you are in a jungle but in minutes everyone and everything had to look immaculate– we had to be dressed and washed standing next to our perfectly made beds.

Inside 'the homes', the ideal for children's self-governance was compromised and achieved through qualities rather more pertinent to the loathed capitalism. Incongruously, the characteristics of capitalism and that of survival of the fittest were rampant in children's dormitories.

> We were made to steal bread from the kitchen, hiding it under clothing or in our pockets; so that when the evening came, we would give this to the older children in our bedrooms. If we told an educator about what was happening, we would be punished by the older children. The older children forced the younger ones to put wet clothes under their bed sheets and sleep on them throughout the night so that the clothes could be 'flattened' by their body's heat in the morning. There were children with diseased kidneys, who fell into terrible crises. Nobody checked whether children were bedwetting or whether something else was going on.

But who else would be in a greater need of salvation, disciplining and civilising than the children of the *tsigani*? The main goal of 'the home' was to raise a person in whom the norms of socialist morals turned into personal beliefs, but the children were also programmed to mute negative experiences; there was no alternative. The rules removed much of the need for interaction, leaving some of them feeling highly vulnerable and alone. 'The homes' were perceived to house 'society's dregs' (Ball 1993: 246) – the children whose parent was the state. This is what Temi (age 59) told me:

> One day we were taken to the seaside on an excursion and some of the children with families and who didn't live in the home decided to go buy some souvenirs without informing the teacher. The teacher got very angry, and instead of telling them off when they returned, he took me in front of everyone and slapped me to show the rest of the children what was going to happen to them if they did this again. I cried so much not only because of the slap but because there was no one there to defend me.

Paradoxically, the state was supposed to look after these children, yet their status as 'children of the state' signalled to the local community, both Roma and non-Roma, to the authorities, to the schools, the employers, to their peers that whatever upbringing they received was always going to be inadequate. Julian lived in different homes for eighteen years. When he left the institution for university, he encountered hostility from what were supposed to be his Roma relatives.

> People wanted nothing to do with one, a *tsiganin*, and two, a child of the state. When I finally met my real relatives in the Roma neighbourhood, I was not accepted there either. I was an imposition, a stranger. They didn't know me; I didn't know them either. My birth mother had died, and I was not on anyone's mind. The only thing I had left was the education that the state gave me.

Still, the state was the only salvation. Violeta saw the director of 'the home' as her 'second mother', someone who helped her to get into university and find a job. She felt that she owed the state not only for her access to education, accommodation and food but also the vital relationships she formed with staff and peers. Somehow to be a 'child of the state' represented both a privilege and a missed opportunity. The state was both de-personified and disembodied political representation, and an embodied, emotional-relational idea represented by the care staff in 'the home' (Khlinovskaya Rockhill 2010: 232). Eventually, however, the residents were abandoned once again, and the relationship they forged with institutional staff was ruptured when they left the institution. Violeta and Julian were youths who upon graduation from 'the home' were deemed valuable to produce a socialist society. But there were others who were deemed not capable of reproducing the socialist moral citizen ideology, amongst them Roma children and adults, who were destined to go to homes for adults with disabilities, penitentiaries and psychiatric clinics. The state had built, literally and symbolically, its own cementing apparatus, classifications and categories, a care machine with a production line difficult to disrupt.

Changing Homes

The postsocialist period is often referred to as '*Promenite*' (The Changes) in people's narratives. Bulgaria ratified the UN Convention on the Rights of the Child (UNCRC)[5] in 1991, but it was not until nearly a decade later that the child welfare reforms began (Mihaylov 2020). After the fall of communism and throughout the 1990s, state residential childcare institutions in Central and Eastern Europe continued to be generally viewed as an acceptable alternative for children exposed to 'inadequate' parenting. This period coincided with a tumultuous economic and social upheaval for the countries in Eastern Europe and the former Soviet Bloc (Gal and Kligman 2000; Kaneff and Leonard 2002; Pine 2002; Verdery 2003). Unemployment rose to unprecedented levels, inflation was high, food was difficult to come by and the economy collapsed. My personal childhood memories of the time are linked to queuing in front of food stores from morning until evening to be able to buy bread with valuable rationing coupons. Employment activities in the informal sector increased, and those who remained employed (whether in the informal or formal sector) faced low pay, reduced benefits and declining work conditions. The state was withdrawing while people 'retreated to the household' (Pine 2002), and 'everything was forever until it was no more' (Yurchak 2006). The transition from a planned economy to a market economy brought the reduction of state expenditures such as on social services and benefits, and while poverty levels increased so did the numbers of children in care homes. The upheaval was not only political, as the children's homes remained the responsibility of the state, but it was also 'cognitive' because they were no longer a priority of the state's changed ideology and diminishing economic resources (Read and Thelen 2007).

Like other Eastern European countries, Bulgaria also commenced the removal of symbols of the former regime. These were monuments and statutes of Lenin and the mausoleum of the first communist prime minister Georgi Dimitrov and others, which were considered incommensurable with the 'post-socialist sensibilities' (Kelleher 2009). However, other architectural and design remnants of the communist era, such as the large care homes, government buildings and concrete apartment blocks (*panelki*) survived. Indeed, the memory of these 'homes', symbols of an era characterised by massive building efforts, all built in the name of care for the socialist citizen, still lingers today. Nasko, now in his early 40s, who lived in a care home in the 1990s remembers the transition period:

> Suddenly, all the staff in the home got worried about their jobs. We said goodbye to the assistant cook, to the cleaner, to the driver because they were made redundant. The food was little. At school, no one cared anymore whether we studied or not. People had other problems to think about. The children from the home were on nobody's radar.

Leading international NGOs began working in Bulgaria to introduce different models of child protection. The state's inability to afford sufficient financial commitment combined with less emphasis on local context relevance by international donors and NGOs led to patchy and non-implementable models of childcare (Mihaylov 2020). Increasingly in the 2000s, media stories began to reveal the poor state of childcare institutions and the horrific incidents of child abuse. Media investigations uncovered the state of children in care in Romania's orphanages,[6] and a BBC documentary on Bulgaria's abandoned children[7] exposed an inhuman system of care for children with disabilities. This resulted in an international outcry in response to the images of malnourished and mistreated children. Several international organisations commenced lobbying the Bulgarian government, and the process of 'deinstitutionalisation',[8] a period of reforms related to the closure of institutions, began. By the time I conducted research with care residents, Bulgaria had adopted a National Strategy 'Vision for deinstitutionalization of children in the Republic of Bulgaria', and the NGO I worked for was providing advice to the government for its care system reform. The research access was secured by my employer, who was interested in finding out more information about Roma children and their identification preferences, which in turn was going to support actions towards reuniting children with birth families, foster care placements and adoption.

The process of deinstitutionalisation represented an enormous change for the staff in the institutions and for the state overall. This change was talked about, resisted and even mourned in nostalgic terms. One of the directors of a previously baby 'home' and now a kindergarten told me:

> We used to have many more children than we have now. But these were different times. Now the government strategies and European investments are not doing much for the children and their future. The so-called deinstitutionalisation is a good idea, but an impossible one to achieve in my opinion. Foster care and adoption all sound well, but this is at the expense of the children themselves. We all want the children to be out as soon as possible, so we fill in the forms, and that's how it is done on paper. But who cares whether the birth family, foster care or adoptive parents are capable enough to look after these children? If we compare the children's outcomes now with the outcomes we used to achieve in pre-democracy times we will be ashamed.

The director's nostalgia for past times (Berdahl 1999) was almost visceral, and it was as if the yearning for what was now unattainable could be observed in the kindergarten building. This kindergarten used to house one hundred and fifty children split into different groups. Such buildings were intended to free women to work and to educate young children as the future vehicles of socialism implementation. One side of the building was uninhabited, dust had settled on the old furniture and the walls were covered with ornate portraits of ex-dignitaries. Still larger than what was needed for two playgroups of fifteen children each, the inhabited part of the building was freshly painted, and the dark corridor walls were decorated in children's paintings. If nostalgia is about different forms of remembrance (Todorova and Gille 2012), this building may well have served as a memorial, a symbol of past and present, old and new, socialism and postsocialism. Perhaps, the director's nostalgia was about belonging, the position of influence she used to have and the pride in producing the future of the state.

Martin (age 5), who was attending the same kindergarten, told me that he liked the picture on one of the books I had brought with me. He pointed to the blond smiley boy on the cover and said:

> I like him. My hair is black. I would like to have yellow hair like him. Sasho [one of the older children] colours his hair, and his hair is yellow. My mummy put black paint on my skin and on my hair. My mummy lives with *tsiganite*. They are black and they made me black too.

His teacher seemed somewhat embarrassed and corrected him quickly:

> Don't say this, Martin. There are no *tsigani*. [Then she turned to me] Children know that they are different from an early age. Martin's mother left him with her mother and went to work in Germany. They have children and never look after them. So, when the grandmother passed away, he was given to us.

With the fall of communism the 'kinning' of Roma children seemed to be of no interest to the state anymore. Care became private again and needed to be returned to the family domain or elsewhere outside of state function, to the mothers specifically. Care could now be openly ethnicised and gendered. Suddenly, identification differences – be they in terms of race, gender, class and age – became more apparent in people's everyday expressions. The end of the collectivist era also brought higher bureaucratic requirements of care staff, social workers and other state agents. Whereas socialism, mostly on an ideological level, attempted to erase all differences between people for the common good, the neoliberalisation of postsocialist times, this new economic realm of individual survival, did not demand the individual to become a member of the future proletariat.

No More 'Mother-Heroines'

In socialist times, mothers were encouraged to produce the proletariat of the nation, in other words, to have more children and to become *mnogodetni majki* (mothers of multiple children). These so called 'Mother-Heroines' (Bridger, Kay and Pinnick 2005) were awarded the title for raising large families to increase birth rates and improve demographic development. The heroic mothers were also awarded medals (see figure 5.1). However, in postsocialist times the higher Roma birth rate (Tomova 2008) came to be seen as a danger to the nation's future. Whereas before the increased 'reproduction of the body' was necessary for the demographic and ideological

Figure 5.1. Medal for mothers of multiple children. © Iliana Sarafian.

development of the nation, now the excessiveness of Roma reproduction had to be limited for the survival of the nation. This demographic threat was also the concern of the social worker Ms Irinina, whom I met through my research for the NGO I worked for.

> As a social worker with over fifteen years of experience, I see more Roma children in my practice than at any other time. The level of poverty I see is indescribable and yet they continue to have children. I need to carefully think every single day about whether these children should be taken away or be left with their parents. If you don't have enough money to eat, why would you have children? Their homes don't have heating, electricity or any basic amenities. How could someone raise children in these conditions? It is irresponsible if we continue their dependence on the state by giving them social assistance ... They need to have jobs and education to contribute to society.

Ms Irinina had the state's legal and moral authority, social position, education, access to information and connectedness to other state institutions. She could authorise the use of administrative and bureaucratic procedures legitimately and on moral terms (Fassin 2015), including by placing children in care. She could also decide to recommend further social support to families, social benefits, help with accommodation and employment. The ethnicised nature of social benefits, however, directed her attention, work and accountability towards preventing Roma dependence on the state. Needless to say, the number of resources and the time needed for administrative procedures, foster care arrangements and judicial and other services incurred more bureaucracy and most importantly were not always 'in the best interest of the child' – the very principle that Ms Irinina was meant to follow. Similar patterns in child protection case studies in England conclude that although there are instances in which child protection measures may indeed be in the best interest of Traveller children, enforcing individual moralities, 'intuition, sentiment and tacit knowledge rather than empirically and theoretically informed judgement' (Allen and Riding 2018: 6). Constructions of what constitutes appropriate care, 'good' or 'bad' motherhood and parenthood, in addition to the stereotypical view of 'excessive childbearing', or because 'it's in their culture' needs further investigation (Allen and Hamnett 2022).

One of my research tasks was also to reach out to Roma parents whose children were in care. Throughout the interviews, I heard about their inability to cover expenses such as accommodation costs, the prejudice of social protection professionals, and the lack of transportation and health care access – all reasons for taking Roma children into care (European Roma Rights Centre 2011). Consider Maria's and Ana's stories, whom I met in Radost and Sastipe respectively.

Maria firmly believed that her two young children should remain with her, despite the warning from the social services that they would be placed in residential care unless her social situation changed.

> Unpaved roads, dust, noise ... barefoot children roaming in the street ... houses that don't have good furniture ... this is what the social services see. But this is our life, this is our place, this is our home and our children, this is us ... they cannot change us by taking our children away.

She was a single mother who struggled to provide for her children. Her partner left when she was pregnant with her second child. Maria's mother helped her with the limited resources she had, but it was still impossible to find enough money for food, clothes and shoes. Maria had to find a job urgently. This provision of material resources counted as 'good parenthood', and the placement of children in care was regarded as the traditional response to 'protecting' and 'rescuing' children from harm and 'poor' parenting.

Ana, also a single mother whose child was in care, got pregnant aged eighteen. The father of the baby, who was not Roma, did not recognise the child as his own, and their relationship broke up. When Ana gave birth, a social worker visited her in the hospital and asked her whether she would consider giving her child up for adoption.

> I was a young, single mother and *tsiganka*, and my baby was this beautiful and white child. She later visited me at home and saw that my parents didn't have a lot in the way of money, so she thought I would not be able to look after my child. My son's father isn't *tsiganin*, so she thought that a mixed child does not have a place amongst the *tsigani*.

The social worker recommended that the child remain under social protection observation, and several visits established that Ana did not have the resources to look after her son, meaning she needed income and proper accommodation. The child was eventually placed in foster care. To succeed in motherhood, Ana had to demonstrate that she had the accommodation and financial resources to look after her child.

A study on the over-representation of Roma children in care illustrates that the main reasons for it, among others, are poverty and material conditions, school absenteeism and single parenthood (European Roma Rights Centre 2011). In my research most parents were unwilling to leave their children in care. Often confronted with poverty, illness or social exclusion, parents decided in favour of state childcare, believing that they are acting in the best interest of their children, although many were convinced that institutional care could bring more harm to children (Browne 2009). The parents I spoke to used the expression 'to give [a child] to the home' (*davam na dom*), rather than 'abandon' or 'leave [a child] in the home'.

'Abandonment'[9] as such, however, was commonly used as the reason for taking a child into care by state agents.

Abandoned Hopes

On a cold day in January, over twenty years after my mother showed me 'the home' where she grew up, I was walking up the concrete steps leading to another 'home'. This had been built on the outskirts of town, so as to be away from the main population. Indeed, many of 'the homes' (not only children's homes but also those for adults) in Central and Eastern Europe are on the outskirts of towns or in small villages. Often these 'homes' provide subsistence and represent the only source of employment opportunity for the locals – usually the director, deputies, kitchen staff, cleaners, teachers, drivers and maintenance are all from the same locality. One could easily imagine how the deinstitutionalisation process became 'a danger' to the livelihoods of all these state employees. In fact, job loss was one of the main reasons to oppose the process in Bulgaria as explained in my personal conversations with NGO workers. Whereas before, under socialism, it was usual for a staff member to remain in a job for life in an economy of nil unemployment, now the care staff of institutions needed to find employment elsewhere or work on a part-time basis, an utterly new post-socialist concept.

When I spoke to the director of 'the home', she told me that she had not wanted to see the closure of 'the home' and fought against it because she could not see an alternative for the children. This 'home' was also a source of income for a significant proportion of the local population, not only the direct care staff but the people who supplied the food, the doctors, the dentists and the barbers in her small town. Eventually, she realised that the process of care transformation in Bulgaria was highly necessary, and children needed family care. Now her effort was focused on ensuring that the staff of 'the home' were going to obtain the training required to be employed in other care services, such as family-type homes and early intervention outreach.

The 'home' building was eerily quiet. Deinstitutionalisation had already begun, and a number of children had been adopted, reunited with their relatives or placed in foster care. I was first introduced to the director and the social worker, who in turn introduced me to the remaining children. Come the afternoon, the children were back from school and were supposed to do their homework, but the central heating was not working; the corridor and the children's bedrooms were cold, so instead everyone gathered around the electric heater in the activity room, consisting of old computers on desks, chairs, one sofa, a table and a desk for the educator. The younger children were playing solitaire on the computers, and the older children, mostly teen-agers, went in and out of the room to smoke cigarettes.

Life in the institution revolved around the lack of family, and the children were eager to speak about their lives without kin. In preparation for the research, I had envisaged asking questions in an empathetic, child-led way, thus doing no harm and making sure children could express their sense of agency, voice and belonging. There were many questions that I thought would be difficult to ask, and I remained open to what I was going to hear, see, feel and 'embody'. However, most of the children did not need prompt-ing; they spoke openly, mostly expressing frustration with their birth families.

Here, I present stories of the bereft, tales of longing for a reunion with parents, and narratives of anger, shock and constraint. The children distrust the system of care, despite the material resources provided, and just as the staff freely express prejudices towards 'bad' mothers and children's ethnic-ity, the children object to being called Roma or being the children of Roma parents. I must warn the reader that the narratives in this section are brief, as is my interpretation, which sadly reflects the methodological limits of my research visits to 'the homes', which were challenging to negotiate. What I sought to capture is a snapshot of child protection interventions and their effects on children, in order to understand the micropolitics of the work of the state, how state authorities and governments operate in people's daily lives, and how the state comes to be imagined, encountered and reimag-ined by its subjects as regards care. Although I make an attempt to convey 'the multiple layers of sensibility and intelligibility' (Jackson 1995: 123) of lived experience in a written account, it can be challenging to identify, to gather, to inscribe, 'to bring the ethnographic moment back, to resurrect it, to communicate the distance, which too quickly starts to feel like an abyss, between what we saw and hear and our inability, finally, to do justice to it in our representations' (Behar 1996: 9). I listened, absorbed and made sense, but ultimately it is the very words of my interlocutors that matter the most, not so much how I interpreted them.

> Lilia (age 14): I wonder why my mother abandoned me. I don't know how she looks or how she speaks. My father came to see me when I was little. I liked that, and I would like to see him again. We often talk with my friends here about why we were abandoned. If I could only ask my mother, why she abandoned me … that mad woman that is my mother that had a child and left it in the pit.

> Elis (age 16): I am here because I wasn't going to school; I was causing problems for my mother, and I was hitting other children. It would be better to be at home, but I don't want to cause any more problems; I just want to get through this time and go home. My childhood is running away, my best time is passing.

Nena (age 15): What and who is outside of the home? I don't have anyone outside. All I have are my friends who are here. They are my family. This is sad, isn't it? Why is it that someone would give birth to a child and then leave them?

Mario (age 13): I'm not happy here. I would like to be with my family. Mum is very ill, and I don't have a father, so she left me here. I kept on running away from 'the home' to see mum, but the police always bring me back here. I do things that I shouldn't do, and I am punished for it. I can't watch TV, do sports or be with my friends.

Most of the children did not recognise themselves as Roma, but they were directed to speak to me because the staff recognised them as such. The main identifier was skin colour. Marisa (age 13) had just returned to the care home after escaping from her adoptive parents' home and told me:

My adoptive Mum tells me that I am Bulgarian, but I know I am not. I just know it. People here call me *tsiganka*. I cannot pretend that I am someone else. Why should I live with a family that doesn't like *tsigani*, and I am a *tsiganka*? They want me to pretend to be someone else.

Iva (age 5): 'I want to be white because my teacher will like me better. I think my teacher likes white children better. They call me *tsiganka* at school, and *tsiganite* are not nice.

Christian (age 10): I can't speak in Romanes because the teachers think we hide secrets from them. But Mila and I speak to each other in Romanes secretly.

Mila (age 15): I have friends here and they are my family now. I am not sure what I will do when I grow up, maybe I will become a cook ... then I can help aunty Bozhka (the cook) in the kitchen here.

Not all the children were preparing for change, but the change in their circumstances was inevitable. The youngest children were likely to be adopted, and the oldest ones were going into foster care. Understanding the life-worlds of these children would require full emersion, long-term participant observation and ethnographic accounts that are able to convey the meaning-making of their everyday. Yet even this short report of what the children in the care homes thought and felt is revealing. These narratives may also be a way of experiencing oneself 'not as a creature of circumstance but as someone who has some claim, some creative say, over how those circumstances may be grasped, borne, and even forgiven' (Jackson 2002: 132).

To Conclude

I wrote this chapter to illustrate the fact that there are Roma persons whose identity is shaped not only by the circumstances in the Roma neighbourhood and community but also by the state, within a different domain of 'home' and within different time frameworks. Just as the concept of 'home' can have different meanings, so does identification. There is much more to be included in the topic discussed, such as what happens to Roma children when they are adopted or placed in foster care as well as what happens once and if they are reunited with their families. As such, I would like to suggest that researchers can and should write about experiences from the margins of Roma-ness, be it within state or kinship domains, and employ sensitive frameworks to account for attachment and displacement, for acceptance and rejection. In addition, I illustrated that the current childcare system in Bulgaria cannot be understood without its historical setting and effects on people's understanding of what constitutes 'home', 'good' or 'bad' parenting, the individual and community. I wrote as I did because of the idiosyncrasies that have shaped me. Reflexively speaking, my struggle to interpret the ethnography and the stories I heard, to present what I think I needed to write about, is because I also attempted to understand my quest to recover my own and my family's past, a past that contains similarities to the stories I heard, which are hard and difficult to voice. My deepest gratitude goes to the people, young and old, who shared their stories with me and to those who enabled me to access 'the homes'. Finally, I dedicate this chapter to my greatly missed mother who embodied everything that home means to me.

Notes

1. Information from the research participants under the age of 18 was presented to the child and their guardian/representative. Permission for each specific interview was obtained by asking adults such as public officials, NGO staff, parents and others to sign a consent form. The names of any children and adults included in this work have been changed to provide anonymity.
2. I use 'neoliberalisation' (Springer 2013) to emphasise that these processes were also resisted, rather than being rigidly accepted by the people of the Central and Eastern European region. I am mindful that this split in phases can be blurry and incorrect; however, the purpose of this chapter is not to delineate them.
3. Social orphanhood is often seen as interchangeable with the term 'children left without parental care', but it implies that children are looked after by the state because of social reasons.
4. Institutions existed elsewhere in North America and Western Europe and historically served the same purpose – to provide safety, refuge, food and education to children. In the UK, for example, the rapid increase in both population and poverty in the eighteenth century provoked the establishment of orphanages. One of the

responses to this was the growth of what became known as 'Victorian Philanthropy' whereby wealthy personalities provided for the poor through charity (Higginbotham 2017). Later, children were recognised as having economic and emotional value, and state initiatives were implemented to safeguard their health and wellbeing (Zelizer 1985). Eventually, the state's involvement in childcare was seen as a nonproblematic intervention aiming to improve the social conditions of those children who were exposed to 'bad' parenting, poverty and illiteracy.

5. The United Nations Convention on the Rights of the Child (UNCRC) states that it is the primary responsibility of the parents to raise their children, and it is the responsibility of the state to support parents in order to fulfil their parenting duties (art. 9, 18). The European Union Charter of Fundamental Rights outlines that in 'all actions relating to children, the child's best interests must be a primary consideration' and that every child has the right to maintain on a regular basis a personal relationship and direct contact with both his or her parents unless that is contrary to his or her interests (art. 24).

6. By 1989 up to 20,000 had died in Romania's children's homes. See https:// www.theguardian.com/world/2019/dec/15/romania-orphanage-child-abusers-may-face-justice-30-years-on (accessed 10 July 2022).

7. Bulgaria had the highest number of children in institutions across Europe in 1989. There was an outcry in response to Kate Blewett's documentary 'Bulgaria's Abandoned Children', which followed the life trajectories of 75 disabled children living in the Mogilino institution. See http://news.bbc.co.uk/1/hi/world/europe/83072 56.stm (accessed on 10 July 2022).

8. Deinstitutionalisation is the process of reforming childcare systems and closing down orphanages and children's institutions, finding new alternative placements for children currently resident within their own families, foster families or adoptive parents and setting up replacement services to support vulnerable families in noninstitutional ways.

9. There is no consistent definition in the social work literature regarding what constitutes child abandonment (Browne 2009). However, in some cases, the child's parents may plan to take their children back, and in others, the child and his/her parents may be forced apart by matters beyond their control, such as migration, war, etc. The category 'abandoned' does not necessarily indicate that parents wanted to abandon their children.

CHAPTER 6

GENDERED STRATEGIES
Kinship and State Moralities

Gender relationships permeated much of my research experiences. I reminisce on my first encounters in Radost when my parents wanted to ensure my respectability and safety as an unmarried Roma woman living with non-kin. This job was then transferred to Neli's parents, and fortunately for me, Neli was also in the same 'unmarried boat'. As I settled into the role of a daughter, I was assigned to the women's domain. But I was not seen entirely as a 'complete' woman; discussing sexuality and intimate relationships with me was to be avoided to a certain degree because of my attributed innocence and expected ignorance on such matters. As my parents' oldest daughter, it was normal for my informants to accept that it was necessary for me to interrupt my research in Radost and look after my sick parents.

Later, when I returned to the field as a mother and spent time in Sastipe, I was meant to be a nurturer and conform to the locals' ideals of femininity and motherhood, and it was through gendered kinship practices that I was able to access deeper understandings of gendered moralities and women's aspirations (Pine 2002: 98). At last, I had more access to the themes that had interested me in the first place. My situated approach, motivation and personal problematic played a role in what I have written about here, and what there is still to say goes beyond the limits of this book; indeed, my work is 'unfinished' (Biehl and Locke 2017) as are the identities of my informants and arguably Roma-ness in general. However, by following the main argument of this work and by employing ethnography, I tease out two themes, or rather two life stories, which illustrate how singularity of experience is worth considering when accounting for gender relationships and identity.

The first theme is marriage. Marriage accommodates and represents the culmination of gender and identity performance, and research has focused on this aspect (Gay y Blasco 2012; Oprea 2005; Silverman 1981;

Tesar 2012). Marriage is paramount, and its celebration is full of symbolic cues. But behind the 'performative' character of marriage, I shall show that marriage practices are purposed for the creation of alliances and social networks based on reciprocity and community-based economy, an economy placed or situated outside of the formal state economy yet still 'mirroring' the state because the state is hard to avoid (Pine 2018: 100). Highly controversial early marriages are widely viewed, externally, as a transgression and as something 'typical' of Roma (Tesar 2012). Importantly for my argument, I will show that there are struggles within kin and community that may not necessarily be exhibited but are nevertheless painfully present. Externally, early marriage and having multiple children are often seen as a 'package', part of a 'backward Roma culture', and form the basis for numerous sensationalist media frenzies. From the 'outrageous' marriage of twelve-year-old Ana Maria Cioba (Oprea 2005) to Roma girls who give birth to babies at a tender age, various images feed obsessive discussions of Gypsiness in media, policy, state and nonstate arenas.

The second theme I touch upon is childbearing, again a highly politicised and ethnicised topic. As other authors have done, I shall illustrate that gender and reproduction are primary components of Roma kin relationships, and they affect trust and entitlements (Durst 2011; Engebrigtsen 2007; Gay y Blasco 1999). One does not automatically acquire positions; strategies and meanings are assigned to 'becoming' a woman, a mother, a mother-in-law, or a matriarch (Cupelin 2017; Pamporov 2006, 2007). Female bodies and reproduction can be a model for the unity and distinctiveness of Romaness, with the body symbolising boundaries between women and men, between Roma and non-Roma. But there is more. Under this conflated surface of rituals and taboos, Roma women also navigate within the set boundaries, devising strategies and reproducing meanings. They may often do so because they are left without an alternative, but as womanhood becomes entwined with group identity, women are not only passive and subordinate but they can also be decision-makers. They may not always have agency, yet they strive to achieve it. So, I would like to invite further considerations of the everyday, of the agency of our informants and of the boundaries that we as researchers may be reluctant to cross. While there has been a growing interest in Romani studies in regard to Roma women's activism, feminism and movements (Brooks 2012; Mirga-Kruszelnicka 2015; Oprea 2004) in a highly necessary attempt to place Roma women's experiences into the wider pool of feminisms, I find that the discussion of everyday Roma women, at the grassroots level and beyond, is somewhat insufficient. Perhaps, knowingly or not, we have focused so intensely on the neoliberal meritocracy model of looking for the 'role models', those who 'made it' in a world of unequal distribution of resources that we have forgotten to consider the agency of those whom we may view as having succumbed to patriarchy and discrimination.

Like other authors, I show that by employing certain tactics, sometimes essentialist in nature, the group positions itself differently from the dominant population (Guy 2001; Okely 1983; Stewart 1997) but not only this. These strategies are a direct response to the sense of identity, belonging and personal value of the locals, which they derive from the moralities they live by. The employment of strategic 'mimesis'[1] (Irigaray 1984), in other words, the subversion of the established wider social order, the adhering to patriarchal stereotypes and thereby risking being misunderstood, labelled and vilified, necessitates Roma-ness, but ultimately, I contend, this is done for securing socioeconomic survival and potentiality. By cautiously re-employing the concept of 'strategic essentialism', being mindful that it is reductionist and may generate populism, as well as being useful in deconstructing historical subjugation, I argue that communities that are largely rejected by both the dominant population and the state create their own strategies. The reasons vary: to escape the burden of kinship relationships; to achieve recognition; to reach self-realisation; to survive socioeconomically within or outside structures mirroring the state. The latter happens because there is an 'ideology that undervalues or devalues the domestic domain in favour of a particular public' and a view of the family, or the community, as antisocial, where 'the visible' politics of the state provide social value but the domestic/kinship world, seen largely as the world and the priority of women, is less valorised (Pine 2018: 98). These strategies operate at times under the auspices of culture reproduction and essentialism (and by the same token under constructivism, as I have shown in previous chapters) and are often based on women's roles as 'culture bearers' and 'model in conflict' (Anthias and Yuval-Davis 1989; Okely 1975). However, all of this does not occur without causing an internal community/kin struggle. This chapter can be read in some ways as a continuation of Chapter 3, where I presented the contradictions outside the community/within the state domain regarding education. I turn my ethnographic gaze inside out by seeing how kinship resists the state and its struggles. Of course, I present only part of the picture but one we should handle with some care. The two stories I discuss here are seen as 'typical' by non-Roma, and I argue that they are seemingly internalised, or mimicked (not copied), by Roma themselves.

Marriage

I come back to Mirka's story from Chapter 3. My initial encounter with Mirka was through the education projects in Radost. She was one of Neli's volunteers who helped the younger children with homework. After Mirka's alleged abduction, her volunteering and school attendance ceased. The perceived 'dis-interest' of Mirka's parents in her education once again affirmed that 'Roma culture' is focused on marrying early with 'lavish' celebrations. Roma early marriages, as expressed in Mrs Stoyanova's sentiments, are seen as a cause for high concern not only by teachers but by social workers, politicians and NGO workers (Kolev et al. 2011). It is often assumed that Roma girls are coerced into marrying by their families at an early age and at the cost of their schooling, but there is no research to suggest there are any personal or community benefits in supporting early marriage. In my research the locals, both Roma and non-Roma, seemed to accept early marriage as a 'Roma thing'; in fact, some of them were even singing this. See, for example, the words of this popular song in Romanes (my translation):

> I will make a big wedding. Many people I will invite.
> Refrain: Everyone will be looking at my beautiful young daughter-in-law. They will love her. Dance, dance my beautiful daughter-in-law. She dances and never stops.
> Refrain: I love her. I live for her. A big wedding, a big wedding. There will be a wedding. Many people I will invite.
> We are Roma, we are Roma and Roma we will die. We marry our children early.

Ethnographies may 'traffic in lies' (Metcalf 2001), with ethnographers focusing on socially efficacious themes 'where the mere act of saying or doing something makes it socially true' (Graeber 2012). Anthropologically, we can conclude too quickly that early marriage is always supported by the community. However, I believe there is a dissonance between what is spoken and what happens; it is a metonymy of sorts. Something may be spoken, even sung, indeed internalised, but it may not be necessarily literally true. Is it because Roma culture is 'created by selective choices and oppositions' (Okely 2011: 55)? Perhaps it was this quest for opposition, authenticity and originality, the pursuit to be differentiated from the dominant group, that the locals were exemplifying in their narratives on marriage.

My personal experience of growing up in a Roma neighbourhood had left my positionality on early marriage somewhat wavering between employing activism to stop it, denying it, or admitting that it is a tradition that will not cease; my own parents married early. Here was my opportunity to scratch deeper ethnographically and find out more about the reasons behind the practice. In the process I found a complex web of kin and communal negotiations which were often taken out of context externally.

Practically speaking, it was easier for Mirka's parents to follow the mainstream stereotypes, namely that they supposedly thought of Mirka's education as useless, than having to explain what her honour meant to the outside world. They knew that they were going to be criticised externally, particularly because Mirka's grades at school were promising, yet they needed to succumb to what little was expected of them externally and what 'had to be done' internally. Witnessing their despair in the evenings, within the intimacy of their home, was an eye-opener. The regret and the emotional burden of the situation revolved around crying, being cross at Mirka and thinking of the feud with Boyan's family. Kinship, the 'prime site of trust and affection' but also of 'power, violence, and inequality' (Pine 2018) was taking the role of the state – the police, the school and the social services. The state could not be trusted. Outside the household, Mirka's kin appeared well-composed and disregarded what the school's opinion was. 'Speech act' and performance can be radically different to what the observer hears and sees (Metcalf 2001: 4). Whilst they settled for the external image, acquired a long time ago, of parents who 'did not care much about their children's future', within the community Mirka's parents were bearing the burden of honour as the most important aspect of adhering to the communal morality. Was this act subversive, immoral even? Yes, it may have been to one person's understanding but not necessarily to another's. Mirka's parents were in fact considering their daughter's future, albeit through the communal lens of understanding gender relationships, and this was the contradicting moral of the story.

Whilst there have been attempts to regulate early marriage, such as limiting the practice during socialism or by introducing legal action against anyone who marries a minor (under 18 years old) in postsocialist years, Roma early marriages in Bulgaria and elsewhere persist, although a marked decrease has been reported (Kolev et al. 2011). More importantly, however, they continue to be poorly understood (Tesar 2018). Considering how marriage practices among Roma are of essence for the preservation of the social order, the gender hierarchy is paramount to understanding what influences decision-making. This creates contradictions and moral clashes. But the clash of expectations, ideals and desires can be traced not only externally within the school and state domain; it can be found internally, with kin also. Ideally, Mirka, who was sixteen and hence not far off graduating from High School, would have waited to finish her education and then ventured into marriage. Ideally, Mirka would have been accepted at university. Again, ideally, her husband would have been the only male child in the family who would inherit his parents' house, preferably a dwelling that would accommodate a separate unit for the young couple. These ideals, at times narrated differently, were somewhat shared by Mirka's parents and her school. These were also two different vantage points with one imagined ideal arrival point – Mirka's good future. However, Mirka's marriage caused a moral clash between the two domains – kin and state – and Mirka's future turned out to be a rather more complicated trajectory.

'She must eat bread with honour and dignity in her husband's house' –
Mirka's father told me. Parents had a particular responsibility to teach their
children, both male and female, how important women's honour was. Surely
Mirka's mother took an active role in advising, admonishing and interven-
ing, but it was Mirka's father and brothers who took on the role of guarding
her against going out late and being unaccompanied. Still, why was honour
more important than attending school? Dignity and honour were of crucial
importance; in other words, Mirka's virginity until marriage was intrin-
sically connected to her respectability but not only this. Mirka's virginity,
respectfulness, reputation and shame were not individual; they were shared
by her family and community group. Her respectability was translated as the
honour of her kin, their name, their belonging and their (plural) acceptance
in the community (Gay y Blasco 1999; Tesar 2012). One must note the use
of language. The word 'virginity' (девстеност/devstvenost) was hardly used
when people spoke of Mirka. Virginity per se relates to something intimate,
personal, physical, biological and individual. Instead, both men and women
referred to it as honour (чест/chest), which is relational, sharable, collective
and abstract even. Honour does not belong only to the individual; it belongs
to the communal, the family's 'desire' and ideals; honour belongs to a 'different body' (Gay y Blasco 1997). Gender is central here. since women are
given the role of establishing and carrying Roma-ness through their embodiment of chastity and decency. Mirka's honour had become the centre of
discussion by all. This surveillance of sexuality – that is, discussing wom-
en's experiences and their spaces for agency, empowerment and choice – is
essential (Kabeer 2021).

What did Mirka think? Mirka knew Boyan, her alleged abductor, because
she secretly met with him after school. So, Mirka and Boyan devised a plan
to stage an elopement. Mirka was in love, but she knew that her kin was not
going to approve of her secret boyfriend. Eventually, Mirka let her family
know about her secret relationship and that Boyan's parents were going to
ask for her hand 'properly'. Mirka's parents were distraught. Her brothers
were angry, and her grandparents cried irreconcilably. They had spent years
thinking of her future, including seeing her graduate and dreaming of her
ideal marriage partner. Boyan was not the ideal future son-in-law. 'She is
beautiful as a teardrop. She could have become whoever she wanted to be.
She deserved someone from good *soy* (kin), someone handsome but also
someone who would look after her' – Nevena told me. Mirka was tall, slen-
der and light-skinned. What Mirka's mother was referring to was a standard
of beauty. The lighter the skin colour of a person, the less exclusion they
were likely to face outside the community. Mirka's new husband was dark
and tall, and by different aesthetic standards, he would have been referred
to as handsome. His skin colour, however, was seen as an impediment, a

harbinger of discrimination. Skin colour was not simply a matter of attractiveness, but it was also linked to status. Since Roma are often identified by skin colour, Boyan's 'darkness' was seen as problematic. Nevena was concerned that Boyan would be recognised as Roma externally and that that would affect his socioeconomic position – that is, finding a job – and his general functioning outside the community, which was going to be subject to his visible race. Nevena herself experienced racism because of her darker skin and had internalised the popular perception of being 'dark' as less desirable and equal to lower social status. This was a painful personal reminder of a time when my father, also dark-skinned, used to take me to school but never entered the school gates to avoid other children ridiculing me. This is a conundrum, a contradiction and an injustice but not one that is unique for my informants (or for my family). Widely, beyond the Bulgarian context, this 'politics of beauty' rooted in questions of power permeates many discussions from academia to the beauty industry. Perhaps this can be explained by the concept of 'false consciousness' as internalised racism is exacerbated by the power of socioeconomic forces (Glenn 2008).

There was, however, something more important than Boyan's looks, and this was his current social position. Boyan (age 18) was the eldest child of three and lived in a small house with his parents, which meant Mirka was to share a household with her mother-in-law. In Radost, the general rule upon marriage was virilocal residence, which leads to the formation of extended families, consisting of parents, married sons and their wives and children. Once married, Mirka was going to become a *bori* (daughter-in-law) whose place was in her mother-in-law's house, and since Boyan was the oldest son, he was not going to inherit his parents' house. The youngest or the only son was the one who would remain living in the house of his parents with his wife and take care of them in old age (Tesar 2012). Although at first criticised, the marriage was eventually accepted. Mirka and Boyan's elopement was successful in the sense that it left both sets of parents with no alternative but to allow their marriage. By now, Nevena had to put her criticism of Boyan aside. When she called me to invite me to her daughter's wedding there was no trace of disagreement with Mirka's choice. Boyan had become her kin.

Marriage is essential when discussing Roma kinship and the meaning of relatedness (Carsten 2007). The stability of the extended kin may be more valued than the individual and needs to be protected for practical reasons. Apart from being 'a functional link in the chain' that connects two different families (Engebrigtsen 2007: 79), kinship acquired through marriage is also formed by 'seeking meaning and identity' (Stone 1997: 278), and I would add that it can also be about seeking to exert agency. Mirka exercised agency because she decided when and whom to marry. Her dreams/expectations were not those of her school or in accordance with what her parents wanted for her. Perhaps she was drawn to the status she was going to receive once she entered marriage. Or perhaps the reason was as simple as wanting to become a bride as soon as she could, to be the centre of attention, to be 'Cinderella for a day'. Growing up, she would have seen multitudes of weddings and their full colour, the dresses, the makeup, the celebration and the excitement that the day brought. Perhaps she did not believe that education would enable her to be what she wanted to become – a lawyer. Indeed, logically and sadly, Mirka's chances of creating a life outside her neighbourhood without experiencing discrimination were markedly lower than her non-Roma counterparts. Perhaps she married early simply for love. The reasons were manifold.

What did Boyan think? Boyan was in love with Mirka, and with this came the urgency of establishing a match with her. Mirka was beautiful, from a 'good family' and very importantly virtuous and honourable. Boyan and his family approved of her. He knew what his role was going to entail once he got married. He needed to find employment, look after his wife and save funds for building a home. It was easier said than done. Once Mirka moved in with Boyan's parents, they seemed happy with his choice, but they were not in a hurry to organise a wedding. Weddings in Radost were not private affairs; they were the celebrations of close kin and the whole community. The purpose of the delay was to prepare for the wedding day, which required securing financial resources and organising wedding venues, food and the invitation of guests, who may be abroad, and picking a good time of year to ensure good weather to accommodate a large gathering outside. After all, weddings mark the culmination of a range of activities involved in establishing a marriage alliance and social recognition (Bourdieu 1976; Engebrigtsen 2007). Apart from these practical matters, the delay had another purpose. The passing of time gave the new bride-to-be the chance to get pregnant. Marriage and reproduction go hand in hand. This also reminds me of how kin/community in its striving for reproducing Roma-ness can mirror the state and its need for reproducing citizens (Thelen and Alber 2018). Just as the physical celebrations of *horo* dance loops were materialising in wedding guests' minds, so were the expectations of future offspring.

Marriages mobilise economic activity and property, and they also create alliance networks that operate within a specific space of morality (Daskalaki 2004; Gay y Blasco 2012). Mirka's wedding was an important ritual event. Young and old, women, men and children in the kindred were allocated specific roles to perform, but it was immediately noticeable that women were the organisers, the dancers and the helpers; they were 'the face' of the wedding. Weddings celebrate the ideology of gender and the values ascribed to chastity and women's responsibility to continue the Roma-ness of the community. Mirka's wedding exhibited all the above, including the focus on continuing what was seen as Roma attributes – the dress, the dances, the music, and the crowds – to introduce Mirka and Boyan as members of the community. In fact, the parents referred to the wedding as 'creating authority and respect' (*да създадем авторитет и уважение/da sazdadem avtoritet i uvazenie*) for the young couple, and the wedding guests referred to their attendance as 'paying respect' (уважение/*uvazenie*). In other words, their unit, kin and honour were going to ensure belonging to the group.

Marriages are seen as a means to strengthen relationships between different kin but also ensure that wealth remains within the family (Tesar 2012). Apart from being a sociable occasion, entertaining and enjoyable, the wedding involves economic transactions – that is, exchange of money, property, gifts, borrowing and lending (Silverman 2012) – between the bride's and the groom's families. But this has meaning. It is on this day that the couple and their kin have to be seen as prosperous, so the wedding in a way is less about the emotion and fuzziness of the young couple's relationship as it is about the appearance, the performance and the dream of a life that is not limited by lack of resources. It is as if the celebration is a projected future dream, and it is this future of joy, dance, wealth and togetherness that the kin and guests attempt to perform – a couple, a kin, a community, 'a people yet to become' (Biehl and Locke 2010).

Mirka's wedding was a substantial financial commitment for both her own parents and Boyan's. The number of resources invested in pre-wedding preparations and the actual wedding can vary depending on economic circumstances and the kind of relationship the two families have or want to build with close kin. There is a private expectation that members of the community as well as close kin will provide gifts. Gift giving and reciprocating at the actual wedding is audited and observed as a sign of respect. Anthropologists and other social theorists have long stressed the role of reciprocity in establishing and strengthening social bonds (Mauss 1925: 192; Sahlins 1972). People invest not only in the social occasions of close and distant relatives but also those of neighbours and friends in the hope that this investment will be returned to them. This 'mutual indebtedness' and a way of keeping relationships open-ended results in 'group membership and solidarity' (White 2004). To have reliable kin and community support networks is important, and weddings represent a moment where wealth transfer and gift-giving provide another way to survive. These are welfare exchanges and transactions of informal support networks and mutual acknowledgement based on kinship and friendship and the logic of reciprocity. However, informal networks may not be always reliable. Mirka's parents were disappointed by the financial outcome of their daughter's wedding, as some of the people they expected to give back did not attend the celebration. This informal social network underlines the precariousness of access to formal life outside the neighbourhood and the reliance on internal informal socioeconomic networks.

Marriage can also reflect state ideologies. Kinship re-creates itself 'in opposition to the state as an alternative form of identification and belonging … Kinship may be portrayed as morally legitimate, while the state is portrayed as illegitimate' (Pine 2018: 100). Mirka and Boyan's marriage was seen more as a mutual contract than as a certificate from the state, which they could not obtain because Mirka was under 18 years old. Mirka's and Boyan's relationship required permission from the parents, but it did not require the legitimisation and the order of the state because the greatest amount of loyalty was to family. Where state, in this case, the school, and the communal practice conflicted, it was the communal practice and the kinship that won.

Nevertheless, even in these situations where the state was mostly absent, marriage was not a random matter. The standards for determining a valid marriage were audited by the community. Although Mirka and Boyan were not counted as married before the law, their marriage operated on the assumption that by cohabitating, otherwise acting as married, their union was legitimate before the community. More pertinently, marriage, following the loss of virginity and its connection to the respectability of kin and community, was a way to ensure that the couple was going to survive economically. Living on the margins literally because of the external nature of the Roma neighbourhood and its socioeconomic conditions and because of dominant discriminatory practices pushed the emphasis on marriage as a way of providing an economic partnership for organising biological, cultural and social reproduction (Bourdieu 1976). Marriage strategies as such cannot be seen in the abstract, unrelated to inheritance, fertility, and even pedagogical strategies.

One may ask whether there could have been a different path for Mirka to achieve what she wanted. Indeed, there are many Roma women today, often university graduates, who defy patriarchal structures. One needs to account for class differentiation in the Roma neighbourhood. In Sastipe's Lower Mahala, which was wealthier and had better access to mainstream amenities, early marriages were rare and frowned upon. Young girls were dreaming of their graduation ball gowns and the travel destinations they were going to explore, rather than becoming brides. Later I understood that Mirka, although married, did enrol back into high school and graduated. This must have been challenging to negotiate with kin, but her persistence and choice are commendable. One may ask then why is it that Roma have chosen marriage to make Roma-ness distinct? Firstly, I would argue that it is the history of discrimination and socioeconomic circumstances that have shaped Roma choices. Secondly, we have partial glimpses to the answer through the lens of marriage rituals. Weddings connect the past and the future; they are celebrations of life, honour, beauty and coming of age. Weddings are also performances, strategies and ways to reproduce status and identity, to pay respect and to give agency, albeit in the context of an unequal gender hierarchy; they are also about performing a sense of belonging that resonates with the hope of a new future. Whilst most of the anthropological literature focuses on Roma, the reproduction of Roma-ness and its gendered moralities as situated firmly in the present, Roma kinship is 'resolutely oriented toward the future' (Tesar 2018), and in that sense, marriages are also orientated towards a future 'becoming'. In choosing to make marriage practices distinct, Roma exhibit the universal yearning to 'become' but not as expected and sometimes by resorting to reinforcing essentialist tactics and the perpetuation of patriarchy not unique to Roma.

Childbearing

My first informants in Sastipe were the women in Neli's mothers' initiative. Becoming a mother opened a new world for me. The presence of my baby daughter necessitated many conversations and the building of new relationships. My intention was to study and write about Roma women's lives from the women's points of view and from a common 'standpoint' (Abu-Lughod 2008). So, in this section, I present an individual story capturing power relations, resistance and the search for strong kin networks and belonging. So far, I have illustrated that gender is a primary component of Roma kin relationships; it affects trust and entitlements. However, while womanhood becomes entwined with group identity (not only in Roma contexts but elsewhere), women are not 'passive and subordinate' (Goddard 1996: 15). Admittedly, before I embarked on my research, I viewed this as 'a double burden' (Hill Collins 2000; Oprea 2004), meaning that Roma women are excluded as being Roma and as women; however, I realised this framework did not leave space for women's agency, and the notion of 'women' per se implies a stable, unitary subject, which women are not. In the process of research, I encountered communal practices that can be both beneficial and detrimental to Roma women. So, bearing in mind that women may not always have the agency to choose and act in their own interests, I also looked for examples of where they exerted agency. Women navigate within boundaries and devise strategies, and this is also about power (Foucault 1980). Power is both structured and enacted in everyday activities, and through observing seemingly mundane tasks I wanted to answer one question that had occupied my mind since the beginning of my research. Not only how (through exploring and recording the details of rituals and beliefs related to womanhood) but how childbearing brings about a different status to, a step closer to Roma women's completeness in personhood? There are strategies and meanings assigned to 'becoming' a woman, a mother, a mother-in-law or a matriarch and these provide clues.

On an unusually cold spring evening in April, I heard the *zurnas* and the drums playing as I and other well-wishers, wrapped in warm clothes, hats, scarves and blankets, walked towards Lyuba's house. Lyuba had given birth to her baby. 'What did she have?' – asked someone in the slowly gathering crowd. 'We have a girl!' said Lyuba's mother-in-law, who was giving out chocolates and directing people towards her husband, who was pouring *rakija* (an alcoholic fruit brandy). Another lady exclaimed 'Congratulations! Next year you will have a boy.' When I met Lyuba's mother the next morning, she was worried. 'She will have to be strong now. Her in-laws wanted to have a boy. Lyuba's husband is a little upset, but he will love his girl, I know. Life would have been easier for Lyuba with a boy, but she is young, there will be more children.' I noticed the language used – to have a girl is to have *momiche* (a girl) and to have a boy is to have *dete* (a child). In socioeconomic terms, to have a son is to have an asset that remains and can thus provide care for the parents. To have a girl is to benefit someone else, since upon marriage girls leave the household and become part of their husbands' households. An elderly Roma man who had three daughters and, in his words, had no regrets about this explained to me the gender differences in this way: 'Girls are seen as willows because they can sprout everywhere. Boys are seen as oaks because they stay where you plant them.' Just like Lyuba, her little girl was going to leave her kin one day to become part of another.

Like Mirka's story, Angel was Lyuba's first boyfriend and she told me this: 'He kept waiting for me in front of my school, so this is how we started talking and then people began saying that he is my boyfriend. Sure, in about two months, we got married.' Within a year of being married, Lyuba had become pregnant. She attended Neli's mother's initiative, where I met her, and close to her due date she had appeared worried. Her pregnancy scan had shown that she was going to have a girl, and Lyuba was afraid that Angel would leave her. She had seen a message on his phone from an unrecognised number; it was someone she assumed was another woman asking to meet him at a nearby café. She believed that if she had a son this would make her position stronger within Angel's family. Going back to her parents' home was unthinkable for her, especially now that she was going to have a child. I saw Lyuba often in the mothers' group, and when her little girl was about three months old, she began planning for her second child: 'I must have a son next time. I need my miracle.' Lyuba knew that if she was to save her marriage and position within Angel's kin she had to give them an heir, and she was on a mission to do exactly this.

Although childbirth is certainly a universal life-changing event, it is also shaped by how women who give birth are viewed by others. Child-bearing brought about not only Lyuba's positioning in terms of Roma communal understanding, but it also brought stigma externally from the non-Roma world. The communal internal focus on childbearing is taken as (mis)representation of Roma women. Indeed, anyone that has multiple children in the Bulgarian context has come to be associated with Roma and represents the antithesis of Bulgarian-ness. Just as Roma marriage is highly politicised so is childbearing. While childbirth is essential for belonging to the 'community', it also represents an exclusion from citizenship because Roma are commonly seen as the representation of degradation, a 'men-ace' (Stewart 2012), producing children on the back of the nation (Tomova 2009). Roma women are presented as 'breeding machines' and 'stray bitches' (Pamporov 2013, 2016), working against the reproduction of the nation. They embody what is seen as anti-nation. Whilst Bulgaria has grad-ually reached the status of the country with the fastest shrinking population in the world – although the country is not the only state experiencing an unprecedented fertility dip – Roma are still marked as a population of repro-ductive excesses and dangerous fertilities (Gamella 2018; Vollset 2020). This is against the backdrop of Western European countries being ever apprehen-sive about ageing populations, and countries in Eastern Europe losing popu-lations to westward migration. The ethnic composition of these nation-states has changed, but there is one quality, one category, one topic and behaviour that has been ascribed ceaselessly to Roma women. It is their 'irresponsibly' high fertility. The preoccupation with the 'purity' of the race (also the pre-occupation of eugenics) puts emphasis on the sexual relationships between Roma as 'dangerous', with the 'polluting' fertility of Roma women framed in nationalist discourses as a threat to the future of the Bulgarian state not only by politicians; it trickles down to schools, state offices and hospitals.

It was past midnight when Lyuba reached the hospital. The midwife on the night shift saw Lyuba and her mother-in-law at the door and had told her to wait until the morning. Women, usually mothers and mothers-in-law, accompany the pregnant Roma woman for her scans, health checks and birth. Women's reproductive physiology is usually, but not always, a secret from males. Lyuba could not tell anyone else apart from her mother-in-law that she was going into labour, since, first, this was a taboo subject to discuss with other members of the family, and second giving birth was related to shame, pollution and sexual relations. Lyuba did not have an identity card with her, and the midwife refused to admit her to the delivery unit until she had proof of identity. The mother-in-law had to go back home and look for Lyuba's identity card while she waited in the corridor. This is what Lyuba shared with me:

My waters broke on our way to the hospital, and I could feel the head of the baby coming through, so I began screaming at the top of my voice. I didn't care anymore. The midwife was furious, but she took me in. She shouted at me to push otherwise she would hit me, and she began slapping me on the face. I gave birth quickly, but my face was so painful afterwards. She left me on my own with no clothes in the delivery room until the morning when the doctor came. I asked for painkillers, but he laughed at me and said that when the *tsiganina* (the Gypsy man) and I were making the baby I was not crying, so now I had to endure the pain.

Childbirth presents itself as an opportunity for the state to control, limit and regulate women's bodies to achieve a certain quality of nation, its health, education and aptitude to achieve (Ginsburg and Rapp 1995). While Bulgarian non-Roma women are targeted by pronatalist discourses, Roma women's reproductive actions elicit political, moral and expert scrutiny, so Roma reproductive vitality and the young Roma population are seen 'as a problem but never as an opportunity' (Gamella 2018: 59). Roma reproduction represents a symbolic crossing of borders as 'the nation is reproduced through women's bodies', but it cannot be reproduced by Roma women. 'Ain't they women?' (hooks [1981] 2014). Ironically, Roma women, who are also Bulgarian citizens, give birth to Bulgarian children who are still seen as foreign. In a way, Roma women threaten the nation by destabilising nationhood and producing insider foreigners from within.

During postsocialism, the retreat of the impoverished state from the private/kin domain became apparent again, as the change of regimes affected the reproduction patterns of the population. After 1989, childbirth and childcare became openly ethnicised and gendered, as the higher Roma birth rate 'endangered' the nation's future (Durst 2011: 13; Ringold 2005; Tomova 2009). Examples of state policies and regulations – such as maternity pay, child benefits, nursery fee subsidies, the requirement to have a birth certificate or identity card in order to give birth in a hospital – confirm the legal and ethical status of the citizen but represent a direct intervention by the state in managing its population and economic production. Roma women's dangerous 'reproduction of the future' (Strathern 1992) warrants action towards state policies and social benefits that are constantly reformulated and controlled to address them, as they deserve to receive such privileges. Durst, for example, rejects the two mainstream explanations for higher birth-rates circulating in public imagination: first, that Roma women have more children to benefit from social assistance, and second that it is 'in their culture' (Durst 2002). Roma-ness may depend on Roma women for its reproduction, but it is not Roma-ness (or Gypsiness) that can explain the differences in fertility between Roma and non-Roma.

This reproduction anxiety transpires also in academic research. Medical research abounds with literally hundreds of academic articles on Roma fertility, activism, family planning and policy. This process is described as the 'gypsyisation' (*tsiganizatsiya*) of the nation and its decrease of quality human capital (Gamella 2018: 58). Although there is a focus on fertility in statistical and nation-building terms, there is not much analysis as to why Roma women have more children, and by the same token why some of them do not have more children or do not have children at all. Since reproduction is a key element of gender ideologies, and I have so far illustrated this, there is limited social science critique on the gendered experiences of reproduction as told by Roma women. The bulk of the literature is found in policy reports and research, mainly in terms of human rights and activism, that have accounted for the forced sterilisations of Roma women that occurred in former Czechoslovakia (Albert and Szilvasi 2017). The subject of reproduction also carries stereotypes among medical professionals (Kühlbrandt 2017). If reproduction is seen as essential for the continuation of Roma-ness but is also a burden on the nation-state, it needs further elaboration in research.

If we are to talk about Roma women and their agency and choice, the subject of reproduction cannot be avoided. Lyuba did give birth to her 'miracle' son. For her, becoming a mother of a son was an achievement and provided status; it was going to establish her position in her husband's kin. But sadly it did not, because her relationship with Angel had disintegrated. Becoming a single mother was never in her plans, and although marriages may seem to be 'done on a whim' (Tesar 2012), and as controversial and frowned upon as they can be, they are also an expression of a capacity 'to aspire' (Appadurai 2004), not in mainstream terms but within the constraints of the kinship and community norm. Lyuba's only focus now was her two children, whom she needed to look after as and however she could. It was as if her life was in the present but firmly oriented and lived through her children's futures. She dreamed through them. Perhaps Nevena, Mirka's mother, also saw her future through Mirka's future, and its disruption caused incredible heartache. The future or their children's future remained a central theme in the narratives of the women in my research. Where there was no chance for self-realisation the only hope left was the potentiality of their children, the next generation that was going to live a life better than the one they had.

We, as anthropologists, are obsessed with the past and the present because 'anthropology is fundamentally concerned with the continuity of tradition and culture', but we tend to 'shortchange the future' in our efforts to recover the past and narrate the present (Bryant and Knight 2019: 3). Even in the cases where the past is not talked about and the present seems like an inescapable reality, as in the case of my Roma informants, it was the human capacity to aspire, the dreams of a better future, the strife to become, that provided the answers I was looking for. So, why is it that Roma women's motherhood is related to the reproduction of Roma-ness? The answer for me lies in the process of becoming, which relates to the future of the individual as well as to his/her immediate community's future. Women's childbearing reproduces exactly this – children as potential better futures and becoming.

To Conclude

Gender relationships permeated my fieldwork. Women were the ones who mostly associated with the world outside the neighbourhood and with state actors such as teachers, social workers, doctors and others. But accounting for their role inside kinship relationships is also important. Here I presented only an attempt at 'translating' Roma women's worlds (Behar 2003) in comparison to the many forms of identification and negotiations of womanhood that exist within and outside Roma communities. There is a growing number of Roma women who defy popular stereotypes and whose everyday lives are worth exploring. Here I deviated from illustrating examples of the highly sought-after role models and elites that challenge the status quo and the perceived 'Roma-ness' by choosing, not without my doubts and struggles, to focus on two life stories that are seen as ordinary, as 'typical' and 'everyday'. I did not want to deny the existence of the stories that otherwise would attract much attention, controversy and labelling in mainstream populist imaginations because they also provide answers to questions of personhood, identity, morality, choice, struggles, hopes and becoming.

Note

1. Spivak takes the 'mimesis' concept further and presents essentialising as 'strategic' (Spivak 1996) to serve a purpose, not without risking marginalisation. Spivak recognised the inappropriate use of 'strategic essentialism' after she coined the concept to warn against the justification of pernicious actions (Kurzwelly, Rapport and Spiegel. 2020). Kóczé and colleagues employ Spivak's subaltern studies to assert that its use may generate controversies because it imposes unification and homogeneity (Kóczé et al. 2018). More recently, there have been suggestions of a shift towards moving beyond the essentialism versus constructivism debate in Romani studies and the proposal of understanding Roma agency 'through the lens of mimicry', not simply as 'copying' or opposing but as a way of subverting the dominant authority (Van Baar and Kóczé 2020).

Conclusion
Unfinished Identities

Endpoints

To conclude this book, I go back to its core idea that Roma identities are varied, layered, and complicated, yet they are also shared and renegotiated in different spaces, stories and domains – state and nonstate provision, history, kinship and religion, the very spaces in, and from which, they can also be excluded. This wide ethnographic scope provides only a glimpse into my informants' lifeworlds (Jackson 2012), but it is purposeful for two reasons. By following the stories of individuals, I brought forward juxtapositions, the singularity of individual trajectories, and circumstances that were unexpected or difficult to understand, talk about or simply needed to be left alone to develop, live on and 'become'. I set out to direct attention to these singular experiences as part of an 'anthropology of becoming' that focuses on both the uniqueness and the commonality 'of human experience as always in flux' (Biehl and Locke 2010: 339). Following 'becoming' and its potentialities has been incredibly liberating as well as frightening because it is human nature to be used to the 'expected'. Uncertainty and ambiguities are unsettling when ethnography stands in the way of theory (Biehl 2014). Of course, theoretical frameworks have limits, and the contradictory nature of life can be interpreted only partially (Jackson 2013). So, what I searched for were spaces, narratives, histories and silences that provided only an entrance into the 'unexpected', which was unsettling at times but still powerful to interrogate, confront and present.

I acknowledge that I set myself the difficult task of not only providing an entrance into the multiple worlds of my informants' everyday lives but also analysing debates about Roma identification that have produced numerous writings, thoughts and discussions. There is hardly any academic writing or policy paper that does not have a discussion on 'who' Roma are. Indeed, the subject of Roma identity can be overtalked and overproduced, and this includes my personal preoccupation with it. Yet, in the process, I have concluded that Roma identification is ever-evolving and contradicts itself. Roma identities are construed alongside and in opposition to the dominant culture, but they can also be chosen, forced upon an individual and a collective, exploited and rejected. Roma identities can be local and global, tied to space, boundaries and transnationality. Roma identities can be imaginary, symbolic and material. They can represent embodiment, symbolism and morality. Roma can strive for agency and speak, question, narrate back and reciprocate (Gay y Blasco and Hernández 2020; Tidrick 2010). This is where we as researchers, writers, observers and participants in Roma lives can make a difference by implementing new ways of thinking, seeing, interacting with our interlocutors and involving them with responsibility. Thus, I am not suggesting for a moment that we need to cease 'writing culture' (Clifford and Marcus 1986), theorising, defending, challenging, being preoccupied with origins and spaces, and even obsessing over Roma identities. However, as illustrated, presenting fragmentation, diversity and commonality can render our storytelling more relevant for the people we study.

Reflexivity plays an enormous role, and acknowledging that the lifeworlds of our informants have the potentiality, the freedom and the agency to become can have an effect on these very lifeworlds that we leave behind us when fieldwork ends. Importantly, we need to acknowledge that Roma identification is dialogical, and it is also a question of our imaginations and writings. As a corollary to this, there are two themes (and many more that will remain a subject for another time and space) that have occupied my mind while writing this book. First, binaries are not always the most productive frameworks in discussing Roma identification (or any other for that matter), and second, considering temporalities as rotational and nonlinear can aid in envisaging Roma future, agency and the process of becoming.

Binaries

Following Narayan's question: 'How Native is a "Native" Anthropologist?', I ask 'How Roma is a "Roma" anthropologist?' (Narayan 1993). The 'insider/ outsider' debate is an ongoing theme in Romani studies as it has been in other areas of study also. From my first ethnographic encounter in the field to the last, I was confronted with identification. This book contains as much of me as my informants. What I presented were themes that have implicated my life experiences since my childhood. My 'insider' status may have given me an advantage in terms of certain familiarities with my 'own' culture

(Abu-Lughod 1988), but it had to be proven, negotiated and accepted. I did not belong immediately despite the valuable insider perspectives. More importantly, again, identity, including that of the researcher, is context and time-bound. Membership in 'the group' does not guarantee nor preclude good research. What is important is that one writes in social embeddedness and self-reflexivity in 'a continuing mode of self-awareness and political awareness' (Callaway 1992: 33).

Each of the substantive chapters of this work began with my personal reflection and how I came to experience the particular theme I discuss. I present my experiences not to assert my 'insiderness' nor my solipsistic Roma authenticity. It is my hope that the result is not a soul-searching exercise to know oneself. On the contrary, including my own subjectivities as an observer, and more so as a participant, as a form of 'radical empiricism' makes 'knowledge effectively conditional upon the nature of this relationship' (Jackson 2012: 23). Taking 'insiderness' for granted would be naive because of this very same notion of knowledge being subjective. By sharing my subjective vulnerabilities as a researcher, I also wanted to suggest that researchers, be they Roma or non-Roma, think of how much more 'profoundly vulnerable' are those whom they study (Behar 1996). There is a body of research produced by Roma scholars who challenge the status quo in academia and question its role in 'sustaining and/or disrupting biased narratives' of Roma (Mirga-Kruszelnicka 2018: 10). However few these Roma voices may be, there is hope that knowledge production can be meaningful once researchers, no matter what their belonging is, can move beyond 'whose knowledge counts' (Surdu 2014, 2016) and acknowledge that relationality with the people they study is paramount.

This brings me to the next binary. One of the underlying themes in the book is that Roma are not a homogenous community. There is also a consensus amongst social scientists that Roma identities are created as a result of and in opposition to the macro-community. As such, the Roma/non-Roma binary has come to occupy academic writing as a permanent framework of analysis. I built some of my arguments around this binary, but without disqualifying it I also illustrated spaces and circumstances in which individuals may identify as Roma or decide not to for reasons beyond the Roma/non-Roma divide. Take, for example, the individual perceptions of education and more importantly how children negotiate these understandings; how Roma who were and are seen as children of the state live everyday life; how Roma can 'act' as non-Roma and why; how Roma leave and/or rejoin the communal way of life; how the 'unspoken' in early marriages is dealt with; and how Roma women find agency in restrictive circumstances. These at times unchallengeable themes have both collective aspects and, importantly for my argumentation, also an individuation nuance.

In our proclivity to defend the communal interests, we risk the creation of an imaginary 'frozen culture, of arrested cultural development', presupposing that such interests can be 'fixed in their most authentic and glorious postures of resistance' (Gilroy 2000: 13). Although understandable and altruistic in origin, this view does not reflect the complexity of Roma everyday lifeworlds. For example, I argued that activism, just as academia, is occupied with the survival of the 'group', the 'community', in pursuing authenticity to counter negative preconceptions of Roma. The tendency is to focus on the individual as part of 'the group', but one can miss important singular experiences that may be unique in transgressing group boundaries, yet they can certainly fit within the wider human worlds beyond Roma groupism. On the other hand, the Roma/non-Roma divide does exist and can be very present in the lives of my informants. The literature has documented that this is the way Roma resist the state (Hawes and Perez 1986; Okely 1983; Stewart 1997), create autonomy and authenticity (Acton 1998) and belong. This 'belonging ... becomes articulated, formally structured and politicized only when it is threatened in some way' (Yuval-Davis 2011: 10) – for example, in strife, to make relationships intelligible within frameworks – and when connecting people within categories, models, theories and 'pure concepts' (Douglas 1966).

There are times and spaces, however, in which the Roma/non-Roma binary is not applicable, even when class differentiation is applied; take for example Tesar's (2012) descriptions of Cortorari 'Gypsy palace-like houses' that contain precious chalices transferred from generation to generation (specifically, father to son) – I doubt that the Cortorari have these for the sole purpose of reinforcing the Roma/non-Roma binary. Judith Okely argued that Traveller-Gypsy culture is 'created by *selective* choices and oppositions', clearly pointing to the selectiveness of choice (Okely 1994: 55). This Roma/non-Roma binary, I believe, we have taken for granted and applied to each aspect of Roma life, risking going back to essentialism versus constructivism, which I detailed in Chapter 1 of this book. I saw ethnography as a way out in such circumstances, as a powerful tool for illuminating the micro, the singular, 'unfinished', 'the non-important' and unexpected, the different identification. Such complex ethnographic pictures of fragmentation challenge binary thinking and its presumed stability. Moreover, tensions and ambiguity can provide productive discussion points – above all when considered in the interests of the people we research (Tidrick 2010).

I also presented tensions between different actors, between domains – private and public and kinship and state – binary ideologies grounded in power relations but in actuality interacting constantly (Thelen and Alber 2018). The state can be emotional and selective in its practices also (Fassin 2015). The seemingly 'unitary category' of the 'non-governmental', for example, turns out to be an unstable category (Lewis 2008). State and non-state alike change policies and appropriate the language of kinship, including through the perpetuation of Roma 'victimhood' (Gheorghe 1997). Yet through this complex web of relationships and objectives, we see local Roma activists struggling with a genuine commitment to the causes they have taken up. Negotiations between public and private, state and kin continue as the state steps in to educate Roma children. Different moralities and viewpoints clash, and the individual stories and reasons behind what is seen as public transgression are lost before the eyes of the very institutions created for the public good in the first place. Who but the children of Roma 'transgressors' would be taken away and be looked after by the state for the common good of the nation? And how do Roma women navigate the public and private demands of gendered moralities?

Kinship and the private category, on the other hand, oppose the state to create alternative narratives and forms of identity and belonging. The morally contradictory actions include and are perceived as the 'dis-interest' of Roma parents in their children's education, the repeated rituals of Roma weddings and the spoken and taboo subjects of Roma women's respectability and childbearing, which are all part of kinship strategies. But ultimately, I argued, such strategies or moralities are behind attempts at socioeconomic survival and go beyond the separation of dominant and dominated; public and private; kinship and state. It is not just the state that the ordinary and incredible people of my research have in mind when they live their lives; it is their Roma neighbours that they want to impress, the community that they want to belong to, the personal dreams they have of a future that they perform through songs, dance, work and life. To take Abu-Lughod's 'writing of women's worlds', Roma, like her informants do not live 'as automatons programmes according to cultural rules or acting social roles, but as people going through life wondering what they should do, making mistakes, being opinionated, vacillating, trying to make themselves look good, enduring tragic personal losses, enjoying others and finding moments of laughter' (Abu-Lughod 2008: 27). Roma are people who find hope and future in their kin, neighbourhood and community – as we all do. These are also people whose lives continue to paint a perfectly imperfect picture that shows one's ability to live in the present while preparing and aspiring for the future.

Temporalities

Throughout this work, I often tapped into historical records to argue that we cannot comprehend Roma identification and choice without looking back at the historical settings in which identity politics operates. Writing about the past deeply influenced my own commitment to the act of giving voice to the histories of my informants. The change of regimes of power from socialist to postsocialist brought change in policies, ethics, public care and, importantly, in moral economies. The values, affects, ideologies and morals of the state changed: from historical attempts at assimilation through the erasure of ethnic and cultural identification to open discrimination, disinterest and exclusion.

I also reflected on attitudes towards the past, often in the guise of 'communal forgetting' (Gay y Blasco 2001), and the emphasis on a 'presentist rhetoric' (Stewart 2004) as strategies for remembering and negotiating the past and the present. I illustrated that while my informants may choose not to commemorate painful historical events this does not mean that these 'affective spaces' (Navaro-Yashin 2012: 12) are not remembered and passed down – through rituals, songs and silences. If the present is a constant reminder of the past, how can this past be celebrated and commemorated? A past of persecution, assimilation and non-acceptance that continues in its various forms in the present cannot be commemorated, but it can be viscerally and ritually remembered, suppressed and controlled. Moreover, the communal collective memory (Halbwachs 1992), even post-memory (Hirsch 1997), may be embodied in this very binary of Roma/non-Roma that plays a role in how my Roma contemporaries see themselves as part of a community and in their acts of resistance.

While focusing on the process of 'becoming', I also found something vitally important missing in the Romani studies literature, which was the lack of focus on how Roma imagine and negotiate their future. This, of course, is something that is lacking in anthropology in general because we are 'concerned with the continuity of tradition and culture' (Bryant and Knight 2019: 3); we tend to neglect the future in attempting to analyse how the past interplays in the present. The future, especially the future of Roma children, was a central theme in the narratives of my informants. The future featured firmly in kinship (see also Tesar 2012). Weddings were celebrated in the present, but it was the future that was being performed. Behind the exchanges of gifts, property and wealth were strategies to ensure the future of the married couple and the potentiality of the kin as part of the community. Moreover, the actual celebration in the present was what people wanted their lives 'to be'. They were literally and symbolically performing and enacting the future. It is this ungraspable potentiality of my informants that I wanted to seize and 'translate' (Behar 2003). The people of this book were striving to become, although not always as one would suppose in conventional and mainstream terms. Most of the time they endeavoured to do so within the existing community structures, moralities and hierarchies, and externally as required, such as with the Roma children in care, whose stories can never be adequately retold because they carry so much burden and emotion. Simply put, there were exceptions. These were women, men and children who negotiated life and wanted 'to become' in a different way, and those singular examples challenged mainstream and communal perceptions.

Finally, my own research is captured by temporalities also. I began this book with the description of the geographies inhabited by my informants, but undoubtedly they have changed in time and space as have the people living in them. Each chapter presented only a limited picture, a snapshot of what are otherwise complex lifeworlds, institutions and relationships. I may have accessed and gazed at a picture of time and space when I was present with the people of my research, but ultimately these realities continue to be lived outside of my analysis. Thus, each of the themes in this work is unfinished and always 'under construction' because circumstances change and so does identification. The 'unfinishedness' (Biehl and Locke 2017) of each chapter is unavoidable, and as liberating or frustrating as it is, the process of 'becoming' shows that the politics of knowledge production in everyday lives is always in motion. This is where this book finishes, but ultimately its core idea is always evolving.

REFERENCES

Abrams, Philip. 2008. 'Notes on the Difficulty of Studying the State (1977)', *Twenty Years of the Journal of Historical Sociology* 1(1): 58–89.

Abu-Lughod, Lila. 1988. 'Fieldwork of a Dutiful Daughter', in Soraya Altorki and Camillia El-Solh (eds), *Arab Women in the Field: Studying Your Own Society*. Syracuse University Press, pp. 58–89.

———. 2008. *Writing Women's Worlds*. Berkeley, CA: University of California Press.

Acton, Thomas. 1998. 'Authenticity, Expertise, Scholarship and Politics: Conflicting Goals in Romani Studies', Inaugural lecture on 11th June 1998. London: University of Greenwich.

Acton, Thomas, and Ilona Klimova. 2001. 'The International Romani Union: An East European Answer to a West European Question', in Will Guy (ed.), *Between Past and Future: The Roma of Central and Eastern Europe*. Hatfield: University of Hertfordshire Press, pp. 157–219.

Albert, Gwendolyn, and Marek Szilvasi. 2017. 'Intersectional Discrimination of Romani Women Forcibly Sterilized in the Former Czechoslovakia and Czech Republic', *Health and Human Rights* 19(2): 23.

Allen, Dan, and Susan Riding. 2018. 'The Fragility of Professional Competence: A Preliminary Account of Child Protection Practice with Romani and Traveller Children in England'. ERRC Report. Budapest: European Roma Rights Centre.

Allen, Dan, and Victoria Hamnett. 2022. 'Gypsy, Roma and Traveller Children in Child Welfare Services in England'. *The British Journal of Social Work* 52(7): 3904–922.

Anderson, Benedict. [1983] 2006. *Imagined Communities: Reflections on the Origin and Spread of Nationalism*. New York: Verso.

Anthias, Floya, and Nira Yuval-Davis. 1989. *Woman-Nation-State*. Basingstoke: The Macmillan Press.

Appadurai, Arjun. 1996. *Modernity at Large: Cultural Dimensions of Globalization* (Vol. 1). Minneapolis: University of Minnesota Press.

———. 2004. 'The Capacity to Aspire: Culture and the Terms of Recognition', in Vijayendra Rao and Michael Walton (eds), *Culture and Public Action*. Stanford: Stanford University Press, pp. 59–84.

Arendt, Hannah. 1977. *Between Past and Future: Eight Essays in Political Thought*. New York: Viking Press.

Asenov, Krasimir. 2018. *Anthropology of the "Ghetto" – Space and Culture*. Plovdiv: Studio 18.

Ball, Alan. 1993. 'State Children: Soviet Russia's Besprizornye and the New Socialist Generation', *The Russian Review* 52(2): 228–47.

Bancroft, Angus. 2001. 'Closed Spaces, Restricted Places: Marginalisation of Roma in Europe', *Space and Polity* 5(2): 145–57.

Barany, Zoltan. 2002. *The East European Gypsies: Regime Change, Marginality, and Ethnopolitics*. Cambridge: Cambridge University Press.

Basu, Paul. 2017. *The Inbetweenness of Things: Materializing Mediation and Movement between Worlds*. New York and London: Bloomsbury Publishing.

Basu, Paul, and Wayne Modest. 2014. 'Museums, Heritage and International Development: A Critical Conversation', *Museums, Heritage and International Development*. Routledge, pp. 11–42.

Beck, Sam, and Ana Ivasiuc. 2018. *Roma Activism: Reimagining Power and Knowledge*. New York: Berghahn Books.

Behar, Ruth. 1993. *Translated Woman: Crossing the Border with Esperanza's Story*. Boston: Beacon Press.

———. 1996. *The Vulnerable Observer: Anthropology That Breaks Your Heart*. Boston: Beacon Press.

Berdahl, Daphne. 1999. '"(N)Ostalgie" for the Present: Memory, Longing, and East German Things', *Ethnos* 64(2): 192–211.

Berliner, David et al. 2016. 'Anthropology and the Study of Contradictions', *HAU: Journal of Ethnographic Theory* 6(1): 1–27.

Bhabha, Homi. 1984. 'Of Mimicry and Man: The Ambivalence of Colonial Discourse', *October* 28: 125–33.

Biehl, João. 2014. 'Ethnography in the Way of Theory', *The Ground Between*. Durham: Duke University Press, pp. 94–118.

Biehl, João, and Peter Locke. 2010. 'Deleuze and the Anthropology of Becoming', *Current Anthropology* 51(3): 317–51.

———. 2017. *Unfinished: The Anthropology of Becoming*. Duke University Press.

Bourdieu, Pierre. 1976. 'Marriage Strategies as Strategies of Social Reproduction', in Robert Forster and Orest Ranum (eds), *Family and Society: Selections from the Annales Economies, Sociétés, Civilisations*. John Hopkins Press, pp. 117–44.

———. 1991. *Language and Symbolic Power*. Cambridge, MA: Harvard University Press.

———. 1997. 'The Forms of Capital', in A. Halsey et al. (eds), *Education: Culture, Economy, Society*. Oxford: Oxford University Press.

Bowen, James. 1962. *Soviet Education: Anton Makarenko and the Years of Experiment*. Madison: University of Wisconsin Press.

Bridger, Sue, Rebecca Kay and Kathryn Pinnick. 2005. *No More Heroines?: Russia, Women and the Market*. London: Routledge.

Brooks, Ethel. 2012. 'The Possibilities of Romani Feminism', *Signs: Journal of Women in Culture and Society* 38(1): 1–11.

Browne, Kevin. 2009. *The Risk of Harm to Young Children in Institutional Care*. London: Save the Children.

Brubaker, Rogers. 2017. 'The Uproar over "Transracialism"', *The New York Times*, 18 May.

Brunnbauer, Ulf. 2008. 'Making Bulgarians Socialist: The Fatherland Front in Communist Bulgaria, 1944–1989', *East European Politics and Societies* 22(1): 44–79.

Bryant, Rebecca, and Daniel Knight. 2019. *The Anthropology of the Future*. Cambridge: Cambridge University Press.

Buckler, Sarah. 2007. *Fire in the Dark: Telling Gypsiness in North East England*. New York: Berghahn Books.

Callaway, Hellen. 1992. 'Ethnography and Experience: Gender Implications in Fieldwork and Texts', in Judith Okely and Hellen Callaway (eds), *Anthropology and Autobiography*. London: Routledge.

Candea, Matei. 2007. 'Arbitrary Locations: In Defence of the Bounded Field-Site', *Journal of the Royal Anthropological Institute* 13(1): 167–84.

Carsten, Janet. 2000. *Cultures of Relatedness: New Approaches to the Study of Kinship*. Cambridge: Cambridge University Press.

———. 2007. *Ghosts of Memory: Essays on Remembrance and Relatedness*. Oxford: Wiley-Blackwell.

Clark, Colin. 2008. 'Introduction Themed Section Care or Control? Gypsies, Travellers and the State', *Social Policy and Society* 7(1): 65–71.

Clifford, James, and George Marcus. 1986. *Writing Culture: The Poetics and Politics of Ethnography*. Berkeley and Los Angeles, CA: University of California Press.

Connerton, Paul. 2008. 'Seven Types of Forgetting', *Memory Studies* 1(1): 59–71.

Crenshaw, Kimberle. 1991. 'Mapping the Margins: Intersectionality, Identity Politics, and Violence against Women of Color', *Stanford Law Review* 43: 1241–99.

Cupelin, Ekaterina. 2017. 'The Kalaydji Roma: Encountering Self, State and Other', Ph.D. dissertation. Geneva: Geneva Graduate Institute of International and Development Studies.

Daskalaki, Ivi. 2004. 'Experiencing Distinctiveness at the Margins of the School: Relatedness, Performance and Becoming a Greek Gypsy', Ph.D. dissertation. Goldsmiths College, University of London.

Deleuze, Gilles. 1995. *Negotiations, 1972–1990*. New York: Columbia University Press.

Derrida, Jacques. 1996. *Archive Fever: A Freudian Impression*. Chicago: University of Chicago Press.

Donahoe, Brian, and Joachim Otto Habeck. 2011. *Reconstructing the House of Culture: Community, Self, and the Makings of Culture in Russia and Beyond*. New York: Berghahn Books.

Douglas, Mary. 1966. *Purity and Danger: An Analysis of Concepts of Pollution and Taboo*. London: Routledge Classics.

Dunajeva, Jekaterina. 2014. '"Bad Gypsies" and "Good Roma": Constructing Ethnic and Political Identities through Education in Russia and Hungary', Ph.D. dissertation. Oregon: University of Oregon.

———. 2017. 'Education of Roma Youth in Hungary: Schools, Identities and Belonging', *European Education* 49(1): 56–70.

Durst, Judit. 2002. 'Fertility and Childbearing Practices among Poor Gypsy Women in Hungary: The Intersections of Class, Race and Gender', *Communist and Postcommunist Studies* 35(4): 457–74.

———. 2011. 'What Makes Us Gypsies, Who Knows ... ?! Ethnicity and Reproduction', in Michael Stewart and Marton Rovid (eds), *Multi-disciplinary Approaches to Romany Studies*. Central European University Press, pp. 13–34.

Durst, Judit, and Zsanna Nyíro. 2018. 'Constrained Choices, Enhanced Aspirations: Transnational Mobility, Poverty and Development: A Case Study from North Hungary', *Szociológiai Szemle* 28(4): 4–36.

Durst, Judit, Anna Fejős and Zsanna Nyíro. 2014. 'I Always Felt the Odd One Out: Work-Life Balance among Graduate Romani Women in Hungary', *Acta Ethnographica Hungarica* 59(1): 165–90.

Engebrigtsen, Ada. 2007. *Exploring Gypsiness: Power, Exchange and Interdependence in a Transylvanian Village*. Oxford: Berghahn Books.

———. 2015. 'Educating the Roma: The Struggle for Cultural Autonomy in a Semi-Nomadic Group in Oslo', *Romani Studies* (21): 123–44.

Engels, Friedrich. 1972. *The Origin of the Family, Private Property and the State*. New York: International Publishers Co.

Eriksen, Thomas Hylland. 2002. *Ethnicity and Nationalism: Anthropological Perspectives*. London: Pluto Press.

European Roma Rights Centre. 2011. *Life Sentence: Romani Children in Institutional Care*. Budapest: European Roma Rights Centre Publications.

Fassin, Didier. 2013. 'The Predicament of Humanitarianism', *Qui Parle: Critical Humanities and Social Sciences* 22(1): 33–48.

———. 2015. *At the Heart of the State: The Moral World of Institutions [En Línea]*. London: Pluto Press.

Ferguson, James, and Akhil Gupta. 2002. 'Spatializing States: Toward an Ethnography of Neoliberal Governmentality', *American Ethnologist* 29(4): 981–1002.

Fisher, William. 1997. 'Doing Good? The Politics and Antipolitics of NGO Practices', *Annual Review of Anthropology* 26(1): 439–64.

Fosztó, Laszlo. 2006. 'Mono-ethnic Churches, the "Undertaker Parish", and Rural Civility in Postsocialist Romania', in Chris Hann (ed.), *The Postsocialist Religious Question and 'The Civil Religion' Group*. Halle: LIT Verlag, pp. 269–92.

Foucault, Michel. 1980. *Power/Knowledge*. Brighton: Harvester.

———. 1991. 'Governmentality', in Graham Burchell, Colin Gordon and Peter Miller (eds), *The Foucault Effect: Studies in Governmentality*. Chicago, IL: University of Chicago Press, pp. 87–104.

Freire, Paolo. 1972. *Pedagogy of the Oppressed*. Harmondsworth: Penguin.

Fremlova, Lucy. 2022. *Queer Roma*. London: Routledge.

Gal, Susan, and Gail Kligman. 2000. *The Politics of Gender after Socialism: A Comparative-Historical Essay*. Princeton, NJ: Princeton University Press.

Gamella, Juan. 2018. 'Marriage, Gender and Transnational Migrations in Fertility Transitions of Romanian Roma Women', *Intersections: East European Journal of Society and Politics* 4(2): 57–85.

Gay y Blasco, Paloma. 1997. 'A Different Body? Desire and Virginity among Gitanos', *Journal of the Royal Anthropological Institute* 3(3): 517–35.

———. 1999. *Gypsies in Madrid: Sex, Gender and the Performance of Identity*. Oxford: Berg.

———. 2001. 'We Don't Know Our Descent: How the Gitanos of Jarana Manage the Past', *Journal of the Royal Anthropological Institute* 7(4): 631–47.

———. 2008. 'Picturing "Gypsies" Interdisciplinary Approaches to Roma Representation', *Third Text* 22(3): 297–303.

———. 2011. 'Agata's Story: Singular Lives and the Reach of the "Gitano Law"', *Journal of the Royal Anthropological Institute* 17(3): 445–61.

———. 2012. 'Gender and Pentecostalism among the Gitanos of Madrid: Combining Approaches', *Romani Studies* 22(1): 1–18.

————. 2016. 'It's the Best Place for Them: Normalising Roma Segregation in Madrid', *Social Anthropology* 24(4): 446–61.

Gay y Blasco, Paloma, and Liria Hernández. 2020. *Writing Friendship: A Reciprocal Ethnography*. Cham, Switzerland: Palgrave Macmillan.

Geertz, Clifford. 1985. *Local Knowledge: Further Essays in Interpretive Anthropology*. New York: Basic Books.

Gheorghe, Nicolae. 1997. 'The Social Construction of Romani Identity', in Thomas Acton (ed.), *Gypsy Politics and Traveller Identity*. Hatfield: University of Hertfordshire Press.

————. 2013. 'Choices to be Made and Prices to be Paid: Potential Roles and Consequences in Roma Activism and Policy-Making', in Will Guy (ed.), *From Victimhood to Citizenship: The Path of Roma Integration*. Budapest: CEU Press, pp. 41–99.

Gilroy, Paul. 2000. *Against Race: Imagining Political Culture beyond the Color Line*. Cambridge, MA: Harvard University Press.

Ginsburg, Faye, and Rayna Rapp (eds). 1995. *Conceiving the New World Order: The Global Politics of Reproduction*. Berkeley: University of California Press.

Glenn, Evelyn Nakano. 2008. 'Yearning for Lightness: Transnational Circuits in the Marketing and Consumption of Skin Lighteners', *Gender and Society* 22(3): 281–302.

Goddard, Victoria. 1996. *Gender, Family and Work in Naples*. Oxford: Berg.

Graeber, David. 2012. 'Dead Zones of the Imagination: On Violence, Bureaucracy, and Interpretive Labor: The 2006 Malinowski Memorial Lecture', *HAU: Journal of Ethnographic Theory* 2(2): 105–28.

————. 2015. *The Utopia of Rules: On Technology, Stupidity, and the Secret Joys of Bureaucracy*. Brooklyn and London: Melville House.

Guy, Will. 2001. *Between Past and Future: The Roma of Central and Eastern Europe*. Hatfield: University of Hertfordshire Press.

Guy, Will (ed.). 2013. *From Victimhood to Citizenship: The Path of Roma Integration: A Debate*. Budapest: Kiadó.

Halbwachs, Maurice. 1992. *On Collective Memory*. Chicago: University of Chicago Press.

Hall, Stuart. 1996a. 'Cultural Identity and Diaspora', in Padmini Mongia (ed.), *Contemporary Postcolonial Theory: A Reader*. London: Arnold, pp. 110–21.

————. 1996b. 'Introduction: Who Needs Identity?', in Stuart Hall and Paul du Gay (eds), *Questions of Cultural Identity*. London: Sage, pp. 1–17.

————. 1997. *Representation: Cultural Representations and Signifying Practices*. London: Sage.

————. 2001. 'Constituting an Archive', *Third Text* 15(54): 89–92.

Hann, Chris (ed.). 2002. *Postsocialism: Ideals, Ideologies and Practices in Eurasia*. London: Routledge.

Hannerz, Ulf. 1992. *Cultural Complexity: Studies in the Social Organization of Meaning*. New York: Columbia University Press.

————. 2002. 'Being there … and there … and there!: Reflections on Multi-site Ethnography', *Ethnography* 4(2): 201–16.

Harvey, D. 2005. *A Brief History of Neo-Liberalism*. Oxford: Oxford University Press.

Hawes, Derek, and Barbara Perez. 1986. *The Gypsy and the State: The Ethnic Cleansing of British Society*, 2nd edn. Bristol: Policy Press.

Herzfeld, Michael. 2014. *Cultural Intimacy: Social Poetics in the Nation-State*. London: Routledge.

Higginbotham, Peter. 2017. *Children's Homes: A History of Institutional Care for Britain's Young*. Barnsley: Pen and Sword, Thirteen Penny Stamps.

Hill Collins, Patricia. 2000. *Black Feminist Thought: Knowledge, Consciousness, and the Politics of Empowerment* (10th anniversary). New York: Routledge.

———. 2015. 'Intersectionality's Definitional Dilemmas', *Annual Review of Sociology* 41(1): 1–20.

Hirsch, Marianne. 1997. *Family Frames: Photography Narrative and Postmemory*. Cambridge, MA: Harvard University Press.

hooks, bell. [1981] 2014. *Ain's I a Woman?*, Black Women and Feminism, 2nd edn. New York: Routledge.

Howarth, Anthony. 2019. 'A Travellers' Sense of Place in the City', Ph.D. dissertation. Oxford: University of Oxford.

Howell, Signe. 2006. 'Kinning: The Creation of Life Trajectories in Transnational Adoptive Families', *Journal of the Royal Anthropological Institute* 9(3): 465–84.

Humphrey, Caroline. 1994. 'Remembering an "Enemy": The Bogd Khaan in Twentieth-Century Mongolia', in Ruby Watson (ed.), *Memory, History, and Opposition Under State Socialism*. Sante Fe: School of American Research Press, pp. 21–44.

Huntington, Richard. 1991. 'Introduction', in Peter Metcalf and Richard Huntington (eds), *Celebrations of Death*, 2nd edn. New York: Cambridge University Press.

Irigaray, Luce. 1984. *As Ethics of Sexual Difference*. Ithaca: Cornell University Press.

Ivancheva, Mariya. 2015. 'From Informal to Illegal: Roma Housing in (Post-) Socialist Sofia', *Intersections: East European Journal of Society and Politics* 1(4): 38–54.

Jackson, Michael (ed.). 1995. *At Home in the World*. Sydney: Harper Perennial.

———. 2002. *The Politics of Storytelling: Violence, Transgression, and Intersubjectivity*. University of Copenhagen: Museum Tusculanum Press.

———. 2012. *Lifeworlds: Essays in Existential Anthropology*. Chicago, IL: University of Chicago Press.

———. 2013. *The Wherewithal of Life: Ethics, Migration, and the Question of Well-Being*. Berkeley: University of California Press.

James, Allison, Chris Jenks and Alan Prout. 1998. *Theorizing Childhood*. Oxford: Blackwell Publishers.

James, Allison, and Adrian James. 2004. *Constructing Childhood*. Basingstoke: Palgrave Macmillan.

Kabeer, Naila. 2021. 'Three Faces of Agency in Feminist Economics: Capabilities, Empowerment, and Citizenship', *The Routledge Handbook of Feminist Economics*. New York: Routledge, pp. 99–107.

Kaneff, Deema. 1995. 'Developing Rural Bulgaria', *Cambridge Anthropology* 18: 23–34.

———. 2004. 'Who Owns the Past?', *The Politics of Time in a 'Model' Bulgarian Village*. New York and Oxford: Berghahn Books.

———. 2011. 'Generations, Unemployment and Exclusion in Urban Bulgaria', *Naselenie* 12: 121–34.

———. 2019. 'Neoliberal Spaces of Immorality: The Creation of a Bulgarian Land Market and "Land-Grabbing" Foreign Investors', in David Montgomery (ed.), *Everyday Life in the Balkans*. Bloomington: Indiana University Press, pp. 155–67.

Kaneff, Deema, and Pamela Leonard (eds). 2002. *Post-Socialist Peasant? Rural and Urban Constructions of Identity in Eastern Europe, East Africa and the Former Soviet Union*. London: Palgrave Macmillan.

Kapralski, Slawomir. 2013. 'The Aftermath of the Roma Genocide: From Implicit

Memories to Commemoration', in Anton Weiss-Wendt (ed.), *The Nazi Genocide of the Roma: Reassessment and Commemoration*. New York and Oxford: Berghahn Books, pp. 229–52.

Kelleher, Michael. 2009. 'Bulgaria's Communist-Era Landscape', *The Public Historian* 31(3): 39–72.

Kenrick, Donald, and Colin Clark. 1999. *Moving On: The Gypsies and Travellers of Britain*. Hatfield: University of Hertfordshire Press.

Khlinovskaya Rockhill, Elena. 2010. *Lost to the State: Family Discontinuity, Social Orphanhood and Residential Care in the Russian Far East*. Oxford and New York: Berghahn Books.

Kitromilides, Paschalis. 1989. 'Imagined Communities and the Origins of the National Question in the Balkans', *European History Quarterly* 19: 150.

Kolev, Deyan, Krumova, Teodora Krumova, Alexey Pamporov, et al. 2011. *Preventsiya na rannite brakove* [Prevention of Early Marriages]. Veliko Tarnovo: Astarta.

Kóczé, Angela, Violetta Zentai, Jelena Jovanovic and Eniko Vincze (eds). 2018. *A Reflexive History of the Romani Women's Movement: Struggles and Debates in Central and Eastern Europe*. London: Routledge.

Kovai, Cecilia. 2011. 'On the Borders of Gender: Marriage and the Role of the "Child" amongst Hungarian Gypsies', in Michael Stewart and Marton Rovid (eds), *Multidisciplinary Approaches to Romany Studies*. Budapest: CEU Press.

Kühlbrandt, Charlotte. 2017. 'Containment – An Examination of Roma Health Mediation in Romania', Ph.D. dissertation. London School of Hygiene & Tropical Medicine.

Kurzwelly, Jonatan, Nigel Rapport and Andrew Spiegel. 2020. 'Encountering, Explaining and Refuting Essentialism', *Anthropology Southern Africa* 43(2): 65–81.

Kyuchukov, Hristo. 2004. *My Name Was Hussein*. New York: Boyd Mills Press.

Ladányi, Janos, and Ivan Szelényi. 2001. 'The Social Construction of Roma Ethnicity in Bulgaria, Romania and Hungary during Market Transition', *Review of Sociology* 7(2): 34–79.

———. 2003. 'Historical Variations in Inter-Ethnic Relations: Toward a Social History of Roma in Csenyéte, 1857–2000', *Romani Studies* 13(1): 1–51.

———. 2006. *Patterns of Exclusion: Constructing Gypsy Ethnicity and Making of an Underclass in Transitional Societies of Europe*. New York: Columbia University Press.

Lemon, Alaina. 2000. *Between Two Fires and Romani Memory from Pushkin to Postsocialism*. North Carolina: Duke University Press.

Lewis, David. 2008. '"Non-Governmentalism" and the Reorganisation of Public Action: Management and the Rise of Nongovernmental Organizations (NGOs)', in Sadhvi Dar and Bill Cooke (eds), *The New Development Management: Critiquing the Dual Modernization*, pp. 41–55.

Lewis, David and Mark Schuller. 2017. 'Engagements with a Productively Unstable Category: Anthropologists and Non-governmental Organizations'. *Current Anthropology* 58(5). Retrieved 4 November 2022 from https://www.journals.uchicago.edu/doi/abs/10.1086/693897.

Liber, George. 1991. 'Korenizatsiia: Restructuring Soviet Nationality Policy in the 1920s', *Ethnic and Racial Studies* 14(1): 15–23.

Lindholm, Charles. 2008. *Culture and Authenticity*. Oxford: Blackwell.

Madanipour, Ali. 2003. 'Social Exclusion and Space', in Judith Allen, Goran Cars and Ali Madanipour (eds), *Social Exclusion in European Cities: Processes, Experiences and Responses*. London: Routledge, pp. 75–89.

Malinowski, Bronislaw. 1963. *The Family among the Australian Aborigines*. New York: Schocken Books.

Marcus, George. 1995. 'Ethnography in/of the World System: The Emergence of Multi-sited Ethnography', in George Marcus (ed.), *Ethnography through Thick and Thin*. Princeton, NJ: Princeton University Press.

———. 2012. 'Classic Fieldwork, Critique and Engaged Anthropology: Into the New Century', *Anthropological Journal of European Cultures. Thematic Focus: Europeanist Anthropology Beyond and Between: AJEC* 21(2): 35–42.

Marushiakova, Elena, and Veselin Popov. 1993. *Gypsies in Bulgaria* [Tsiganite v Bulgaria]. Sofia: Club' 90.

———. 1999. 'The Gypsy Minority in Bulgaria – Policy and Community Development', in Csaba Fényes, Christina McDonald and Anita Mészáros (eds), *The Roma Education Resource Pack*. Budapest: Open Society Institute.

———. 2000. 'The Relations of Ethnic and Confessional Consciousness of Gypsies in Bulgaria', *Series on Philosophy and Sociology*. University of Nis Publications 2(6): 81–9.

———. 2001. *The Gypsies in the Ottoman Empire*. Sofia: Litavra.

———. 2005. 'The Roma – A Nation Without a State? Historical Background and Contemporary Tendencies', in Wojciech Burszta and Sebastian Wojciechowski, *Nationalisms Across the Globe: An Overview of Nationalisms in State-Endowed and Stateless Nations*. Poznan: School of Humanities and Journalism, pp. 433–55.

———. 2011. 'Between Exoticization and Marginalization Current Problems of Gypsy Studies', *Behemoth-A Journal on Civilisation* 4(1): 86–105.

———. 2015. *From Dust to Digital: Ten Years of the Endangered Archives Programme*. Cambridge: Open Book Publishers.

———. 2021. *Roma Voices in History: A Sourcebook*. Schöningh: Brill.

Marx, Karl, and Eleanor Aveling Marx. 1891. *The Eastern Question, a Reprint of Letters Written 1853–1856 Dealing with the Events of the Crimean War*. Primary Source Edition. London: Swan Sonnenschein and Co.

Massey, Doreen. 1994. 'Double Articulation: A Place in the World', in Angelika Bammer (ed.), *Displacements: Cultural Identities in Question*. Bloomington: Indiana University Press.

Matras, Yaron. 2002. *Romani: A Linguistic Introduction*. Cambridge: Cambridge University Press.

———. 2013. 'Scholarship and the Politics of Romani Identity: Strategic and Conceptual Issues', in Sia Spiliopoulou Åkermark, Arie Bloed, Rainer Hofmann, et al. (eds), *European Yearbook of Minority Issues*, vol. 10. Bozen/Bolzano: Brill, pp. 209–45.

Mauss, Marcel. 1925. *The Gift: Forms and Functions of Exchange in Archaic Societies*. London: Routledge.

McGarry, Aidan. 2010. *Who Speaks for the Roma? Political Representation of a Transnational Minority Community*. New York: Continuum.

———. 2014. 'Roma as a Political Identity: Exploring Representations of Roma in Europe', *Ethnicities* 14(6): 756–74.

Metcalf, Peter. 2001. *They Lie, We Lie: Getting on with Anthropology*. London: Routledge.

Mihaylov, Stoyan. 2020. 'Deinstitutionalisation or Reinstitutionalisation of Children at Risk in Bulgaria: Prerequisites, Logic and Metamorphosis' [Deinstitutsionalizatsiya ili Reinstitutsionalitsia na detsata v risk v Bulgaria], Ph.D. dissertation. Sofia: University of Sofia.

Miller, Carol. 1998. 'American Roma and the Ideology of Defilement', in Diane Tong (ed.), *Gypsies: An Interdisciplinary Reader*. New York: Routledge, pp. 18–29.

Mirga, Andrzej. 2018. 'Those Who Count: Expert Practices of Roma Classification', *Critical Romani Studies* 1(1): 114–26.

Mirga, Andrzej, and Nicolae Georghe. 1997. *Roma in the XXIst Century: A Policy.* Princeton, NJ: Project on Ethnic Relations.

Mirga-Kruszelnicka, Anna. 2015. 'Romani Studies and Emerging Romani Scholarship', *Roma Rights: Journal of European Roma Rights Centre* 20(2): 39–46.

———. 2018. 'Challenging Anti-Gypsyism in Academia: The Role of Romani Scholars', *Critical Romani Studies* 1(1): 8–28.

Mladenov, Teodor. 2015. 'From State Socialist to Neoliberal Productivism: Disability Policy and Invalidation of Disabled People in the Postsocialist Region', *Critical Sociology* 43(7–8): 1109–23.

Morris, Lydia. 1994. *Dangerous Classes: The Underclass and Social Citizenship.* London: Routledge.

Narayan, Kirin. 1993. 'How Native is a "Native" Anthropologist?', *American Anthropologist* 95(3): 671–86.

Navaro-Yashin, Yael. 2002. *Faces of the State: Secularism and Public Life in Turkey.* Princeton, NJ: Princeton University Press.

———. 2012. *The Make-Believe Space: Affective Geography in a Postwar Polity.* Duke University Press.

Nora, Pierre. 1996. 'General Introduction: Between Memory and History', *Realms of Memory.* New York: Columbia University Press, pp. 1–20.

Okely, Judith. 1975. 'Gypsy Women: Models in Conflict', in Shirley Ardener (ed.), *Perceiving Women.* New York: Wiley, pp. 55–86.

———. 1983. *The Traveller-Gypsies.* Cambridge: Cambridge University Press.

———. 1994. 'Constructing Difference: Gypsies as "Other"', *Anthropological Journal on European Cultures* 3(2): 55–73.

———. 1997. 'Non-Territorial Culture as The Rationale for the Assimilation of Gypsy Children', *Childhood* 4(1): 63–80.

———. 2011. 'Constructing Culture through Shared Location, Bricolage and Exchange: The Case of Gypsies and Roma', in Michael Stewart and Marton Rovid (eds), *Multi-disciplinary Approaches to Romani Studies.* Budapest: Central European University Press.

Okely, Judith, and Helen Callaway (eds). 1992. *Anthropology and Autobiography.* London: Routledge.

O'Nions, Helen. 2010. 'Divide and Teach: Educational Inequality and the Roma', *The International Journal of Human Rights* 14(3): 464–89.

Oprea, Alexandra. 2004. 'Re-envisioning Social Justice from the Ground Up: Including the Experiences of Romani Women', *Essex Human Rights Review* 1(1): 29–39.

———. 2005. 'The Arranged Marriage of Ana Maria Cioaba, Intra-Community Oppression and Romani Feminist Ideals: Transcending the "Primitive Culture" Argument', *European Journal of Women's Studies* 2(5): 133–48.

Ortner, Shirley. 2019. 'Practicing Engaged Anthropology', *Anthropology of This Century* 25: 1–17.

Oskanian, Kevork. 2021. *Russian Exceptionalism between East and West: The Ambiguous Empire*. Palgrave Macmillan Cham.

Pamporov, Alexey. 2006. 'Structure of the Roma Everyday in Bulgaria', Ph.D. dissertation. Sofia: Bulgarian Academy of Sciences, Institute of Sociology.

———. 2007. 'Sold like a Donkey? Bride-Price among the Bulgarian Roma', *Journal of the Royal Anthropological Institute* 13: 471–76.

———. 2013. 'The Anti-Roma Stereotypes in Bulgaria', in Deyan Kolev and Teodora Krumova (eds), *Beyond Anti-Roma Stereotypes: The World is Not Just White and Black*. Sofia: Astarta.

———. 2016. *Local Engagement for Roma Inclusion: Locality Study Stara Zagora*. Brussels: European Agency of Fundamental Rights.

Pelkmans, Mathijs. 2009. 'Introduction: Post-Soviet Space and the Unexpected Turns of Religious Life', in Mathijs Pelkmans (ed.), *Conversion after Socialism: Disruptions, Modernisms, and the Technologies of Faith*. Oxford: Berghahn Books, pp. 1–16.

Pine, Frances. 1998. 'Dealing with Fragmentation', in Sue Bridger and Frances Pine (eds), *Surviving Postsocialism: Local Strategies and Regional Responses in Eastern Europe and the Former Soviet Union*. Oxford: Routledge.

———. 2002. 'Retreat to the Household?', in Chris Hann (ed.), *Postsocialism: Ideals, Ideologies, and Practices in Eurasia*. London: Routledge.

———. 2003. 'Reproducing the House: Kinship, Inheritance, and Property Relations in Highland Poland', in Hannes Grandits and Patrick Heady (eds), *Distinct Inheritances: Property, Family and Community in a Changing Europe*. Münster: LIT Verlag.

———. 2007. 'Memories of Movement and the Stillness of Place: Kinship Memory in the Polish Highlands', in Janet Casten (ed.), *Ghosts of Memory: Essays on Remembrance and Relatedness*. Oxford: Wiley-Blackwell, pp. 104–25.

———. 2018. 'Inside and Outside the Language of Kinship: Public and Private Conceptions of Sociality', in Tatjana Thelen and Erdmute Alber (eds), *Reconnecting State and Kinship*. Philadelphia: University of Pennsylvania Press.

Rajkai, Zsombor. 2014. *Family and Social Change in Socialist and Post-socialist Societies*. London: Brill.

Ramos, Alcida. 1994. 'The Hyperreal Indian', *Critique of Anthropology* 14(2): 153–71.

Rapport, Nigel, and Andrew Dawson (eds). 1998. *Migrants of Identity: Perceptions of Home in a World of Movement*. Oxford: Berg.

Read, Rosie, and Tatjana Thelen. 2007. 'Introduction: Social Security and Care after Socialism: Reconfigurations of Public and Private', *Focaal* 50: 3–18.

Ries, Johannes. 2011. 'Romany/Gypsy Church or People of God? The Dynamics of Pentecostal Mission and Romani/Gypsy Ethnicity Management', in Michael Stewart and Marton Rovid (eds), *Multi-disciplinary Approaches to Romani Studies*. Budapest: CEU Press, pp. 271–79.

Riessman, Catherine. 2008. *Narrative Methods for the Human Sciences*. Los Angeles: Sage.

Ringold, Dena. 2005. *Roma in an Expanding Europe: Breaking the Poverty Cycle*. Washington, DC: World Bank.

Robbins, Joel. 2016. 'What is the Matter with Transcendence? On the Place of Religion in the New Anthropology of Ethics', *Journal of the Royal Anthropological Institute* 22(4): 767–81.

Roman, Bianca Raluca. 2015. 'Religion and Transnational Roma Mobilization: From Local Religious Participation to Transnational Social Activism in the Case of the

Finnish Roma', in Titus Hjelm (ed.), *Is God Back? Reconsidering the New Visibility of Religion*. London and New York: Bloomsbury Academic, pp. 205–16.

Sahlins, Marshall. 1972. 'The Original Affluent Society: A Short Essay', in Carol Delaney (ed.), *Investigating Culture: An Experiential Introduction to Anthropology*. Oxford: Blackwell.

Said, Edward. 1993. *Culture and Imperialism*. New York: Knopf.

Savova, Nadezhda. 2007. 'Community Creative Capital: UNESCO's Intangible Heritage Politics Revisited in the Bulgarian Chitalishte', *The International Journal of the Arts in Society* 2(1): 193–202.

Sharma, Aradhana, and Akhil Gupta (eds). 2006. *The Anthropology of the State: A Reader*. Oxford: Blackwell.

Sigona, Nando, and Nidhi Trehan (eds). 2009. *Romani Politics in Contemporary Europe: Poverty, Ethnic Mobilization, and the Neoliberal Order*. London: Palgrave Macmillan.

Silverman, Carol. 1981. 'Pollution and Power: Gypsy Women in America', in Matt Salo (ed.), *The American Kalderash: Gypsies in the New World*. Centenary College, NJ: Gypsy Lore Society, pp. 55–71.

———. 1983. 'The Politics of Folklore in Bulgaria', *Anthropological Quarterly* 56(2): 55–61.

———. 1988. 'Negotiating "Gypsiness": Strategy in Context', *The Journal of American Folklore* 101(40): 261–75.

———. 2012. *Romani Routes: Cultural Politics and Balkan Music in Diaspora*. Oxford: Oxford University Press.

Spivak, Gayatri Chakravorty. 1996. 'Subaltern Studies: Deconstructing Historiography', in Donna Landry and Gerald MacLean (eds), *The Spivak Reader: Selected Works of Gayatri Chakravorty Spivak*, London: Routledge, pp. 203–36.

Springer, Simon. 2013. 'Neoliberalism', in Klaus Dodds, Merje Kuus and Joanne Sharp (eds), *The Ashgate Research Companion to Critical Geopolitics*. Farnham: Ashgate, pp. 147–64.

Stewart, Michael. 1997. *The Time of the Gypsies*. Oxford: Westview Press.

———. 2001. 'Communist Roma Policy 1945–1989 as Seen through the Hungarian Case', in Will Guy (ed.), *Between Past and Future: The Roma of Central and Eastern Europe*. Hatfield: University of Hertfordshire Press.

———. 2004. 'Remembering without Commemoration: The Mnemonics and Politics of Holocaust Memories among European Roma', *The Journal of the Royal Anthropological Institute* 10(3): 561–82.

———. 2011. 'Introduction: Challenges for Scholarship in the Field of Romani Studies', in Michael Stewart and Marton Rovid (eds), *Multidisciplinary Approaches to Romany Studies*. Budapest: Central European University Press, pp. 1–9.

Stewart, Michael (ed.). 2012. *The Gypsy 'Menace': Populism and the New Anti-Gypsy Politics*. London: Hurst Publishers.

———. 2013. 'Roma and Gypsy "Ethnicity" as a Subject of Anthropological Inquiry', *Annual Review of Anthropology* 42: 415–32.

Stewart, Michael, and Marton Rovid (eds). 2011. *Multi-Disciplinary Approaches to Romani Studies*. Budapest: Central European University Press.

Stoler, Ann. 2004. 'Affective States', in David Nugent and Joan Vincent (eds), *A Companion to the Anthropology of Politics*. Blackwell, Oxford.

Stone, Linda. 1997. *Kinship and Gender: An Introduction*. Boulder, CO: Westview Press.

Stoykova, Elena. 2006. *Ideological Model of the Family and its Crisis in Socialist Bulgaria*. Amsterdam: International Institute of Social History.

Strathern, Marilyn. 1992. *Reproducing the Future: Anthropology, Kinship, and the New Reproductive Technologies*. New York: Routledge.

Strathern, Marilyn (ed.). 2000. *Audit Cultures: Anthropological Studies in Accountability, Ethics, and the Academy*. London, England: Routledge.

———. 2004. *Partial Connections*. Lanham: Rowman and Littlefield.

Surdu, Mihai. 2014. *Who Defines the Roma?* Budapest: Open Society Foundations.

———. 2016. *Those Who Count: Expert Practices of Roma Classification*. Budapest: Central European University Press.

Surdu, Mihai, and Martin Kováts. 2015. 'Roma Identity as an Expert-political Construction', *Social Inclusion* 3(5): 5–18.

Tambiah, Stanley. 1990. *Magic, Science, Religion and the Scope of Rationality*. Cambridge: Cambridge University Press.

Taussig, Michael. 1997. *The Magic of the State*. New York: Routledge.

Tesar, Catalina. 2012. 'Becoming Rom (Male), Becoming Romni (Female) among Romanian Cortorari Roma: On Body and Gender', *Romani Studies* 22(2): 113–40.

———. 2018. 'Marriages, Wealth, and Generations among the Cortorari Roma of Romania: Notes on Future-Oriented Kinship [Mariages, richesse et générations chez les Roms Cortorari de Roumanie: Notes sur une parenté tournée vers l'avenir]', *Ethnologie française 2018/4* (172): 613–22.

Thelen, Tatjana, and Erdmute Alber (eds). 2018. *Reconnecting State and Kinship*. Philadelphia: University of Pennsylvania Press.

Thelen, Tatjana, and Haldis Haukanes (eds). 2010. *Parenting after the Century of the Child*. Farnham: Ashgate.

Theodosiou, Aspasia. 2008. 'Disorienting Rhythms: Gypsiness, "Authenticity" and Place on the Greek Albanian Border', *History and Anthropology* 18: 153–75.

Tidrick, Heather. 2010. '"Gadžology" as Activism: What I Would Have Ethnography Do for East European Roma', *Collaborative Anthropologies* 3: 121–31.

Tiktin, Miriam. 2011. *Casualties of Care: Immigration and the Politics of Humanitarianism in France*. Berkeley: University of California Press.

Timmer, Andrea. 2010. 'Constructing the "Needy Subject": NGO Discourses of Roma Need', *Political and Legal Anthropology Review* 33(2): 264–81.

Todorova, Maria, and Zsuzsa Gille (eds). 2012. *Post-Communist Nostalgia*. New York: Berghahn Books.

Toma, Stefania. 2012. 'Segregation and Ethnic Conflicts in Romania: Getting beyond the Model of "the Last Drop"', in Michael Stewart (ed.), *The Gypsy Menace: Populism and the New Anti-Gypsy Politics*. London: Hurst and Co, pp. 191–215.

Tomova, Ilona. 2008. *Demographic Process Underway in the Large Ethno-Confessional Communities of Bulgaria*. Sofia: Bulgarian Academy of Sciences, Institute of Sociology.

———. 2009. 'The Health of Roma Women: Case Studies in the Town of Kyustendil', *Population* (3–4): 97–114.

Trehan, Nidhi. 2001. 'In the Name of Roma: The Role of Private Foundations and NGOs', in Will Guy (ed.), *Between Past and Future: The Roma of Central and Eastern Europe*. Hatfield: University of Hertfordshire Press, pp. 134–49.

Tremlett, Annabel. 2014. 'Making a Difference without Creating a Difference: Super-diversity as a New Direction for Research on Roma Minorities'. *Ethnicities* 14(6): 830–48.

Trouillot, Michel-Rolph. 1995. *Silencing the Past: Power and the Production of History.* Boston: Beacon Press.

Turner, Victor. 1967. 'Betwixt and Between: The Liminal Period in Rites de Passage', *The Forest of Symbols: Aspects of Ndembu Ritual.* Itaca, NY: Cornell University Press, pp. 93–111.

Valkov, Nikolay. 2009. 'Associational Culture in Pre-Communist Bulgaria: Considerations for Civil Society and Social Capital', *Voluntas* 20: 424–47.

Van Baar, Huub. 2011. 'Europe's Romaphobia: Problematization, Securitization, Nomadization', *Environment and Planning Society and Space.* Brussels: European Parliament.

———. 2018. 'Neoliberalism and the Spirit of Nongovernmentalism: Toward an Anthropology of Roma-Related Engagement and Activism', in S. Beck and A. Ivasiuc (eds), *Roma Activism: Reimagining Power and Knowledge.* New York: Berghahn Books.

Van Baar, Huub and Ángéla Kóczé (eds). 2020. *The Roma and Their Struggle for Identity in Contemporary Europe.* New York: Berghahn Books.

Verdery, Katherine. 1996. *What Was Socialism and What Comes Next.* Princeton, NJ: Princeton University Press.

———. 2003. *The Vanishing Hectare: Property and Value in Postsocialist Transylvania.* New York: Cornell University Press.

Vermeersch, Peter. 2001. *Roma Identity and Ethnic Mobilisation in Central European Politics*, European Consortium for Political Research Joint Sessions on 6–11 April 2001, Grenoble, France: ECPR.

———. 2005. 'Marginality, Advocacy, and the Ambiguities of Multiculturalism: Notes on Romani Activism in Central Europe', *Identities: Global Studies in Culture and Power* 12(4): 451–78.

———. 2006. *The Romani Movement: Romani Politics and Ethnic Mobilisation in Contemporary Central Europe.* Oxford: Berghahn Books.

———. 2012a. *Theories of Ethnic Mobilisation: Overview and Recent Trends.* Leuven: Centre for Research on Peace and Development.

———. 2012b. 'Reframing the Roma: EU Initiatives and the Politics of Representation', *Journal of Ethnic and Migration Studies* 38(8): 1195–212.

Vertovec Steven. 2007. 'Super-diversity and its Implications', *Ethnic and Racial Studies* 30(6): 1024–54.

Voiculescu, Cerasela. 2019. 'Neoliberal Governance, Education, and Roma in Romania', *Sociological Research Online* 24(3): 314–31.

Vollset, Emill et al. 2020. 'Fertility, Mortality, Migration, and Population Scenarios for 195 Countries and Territories from 2017 to 2100: Forecasting Analysis for the Global Burden of Disease Study', *The Lancet* 396(ue 10258).

Warner, Michael. 2002. *Publics and Counterpublics.* Cambridge: Zone Books.

Watson, Ruby (ed.). 1994. *Memory, History, and Opposition under State Socialism.* Santa Fe, New Mexico: School of American Research Press.

Weitz, Eric. 2002. 'Racial Politics without the Concept of Race: Reevaluating Soviet Ethnic and National Purges', *Slavic Review* 61(1): 1–29.

White, Jenny. 2004. *Money Makes Us Relatives: Women's Labor in Urban Turkey.* London: Routledge.

Williams, Patrick. 2003. *Gypsy World: The Silence of the Living and the Voices of the Dead.* Chicago: University Press.

Willis, Paul. 1977. *Learning to Labour – How Working Class Kids Get Working Class Jobs.* London and New York: Routledge.

Yıldız, Can, and Nicholas De Genova. 2018. 'Un/Free Mobility: Roma Migrants in the European Union', *Social Identities* 24(4): 425–41.

Yurchak, Alexei. 2006. *Everything Was Forever, Until It Was No More: The Last Soviet Generation.* Princeton, NJ: Princeton University Press.

Yuval-Davis, Nira. 2011. *The Politics of Belonging: Intersectional Contestations.* London: Sage.

Zelizer, Viviana. 1985. *Pricing the Priceless Child.* Princeton, NJ: Princeton University Press.

Index

❀ ❀ ❀

Ingram Content Group UK Ltd.
Milton Keynes UK
UKHW022150020523
421125UK00006B/63